My Love Is Like A

Edwin Emmanuel Bradford in Paris, 1897 or 1898

My Love Is Like All Lovely Things

Selected Poems of E. E. Bradford

Selected, with an essay on the poet's life and work,
by C. Caunter

ARCADIAN DREAMS
London

Other Arcadian Dreams titles

Edmund Marlowe

Alexander's Choice

Michael Davidson

The World, the Flesh and Myself
Sicilian Vespers and Other Writings
Some Boys

First published in 2023 by Arcadian Dreams, London
Introduction, editing, essay and cover design:
© C. Caunter, 2023

ISBN 978-1-914571-30-5

Contents

From *In Quest of Love and Other Poems* (1914)

From *Lays of Love and Life* (1916)

From *The New Chivalry and Other Poems* (1918)

From *The Romance of Youth and Other Poems* (1920)

From *Ralph Rawdon: A Story in Verse* (1922)

Introduction

The idea to publish an anthology of E. E. Bradford's poetry along with an in-depth look at his life and work was born from a conviction that his talent deserves wider discovery and that his joyous, confident outlook can hearten and inspire today's readers. The Uranian poets in general have received comparatively scant attention and recognition, their work labouring under a stigma of being stilted, saccharine and subpar. While Bradford was not stylistically a modern poet, it will be seen from his best offerings that his merit goes easily beyond the mere historical relevance inherent in his place among the Uranians.

This anthology presents a selection from each of Bradford's twelve volumes of poetry. It also includes the first extensive description of his life, along with a discussion of his poetry and prose and the responses his work has elicited. An attempt has been made to answer a question that has intrigued commentators: how could his open, unapologetic boy-love poetry have been reviewed so favourably by major publications in early-20th-century Britain? A previous, shorter version of this essay was published in December 2022 on Greek Love Through the Ages (https://greek-love.com).

Spelling or printing errors, few in number, found in the original volumes have been silently emended. I thank Edmund Marlowe, novelist and webmaster, Timothy d'Arch Smith, pioneer biographer and bibliographer of the Uranians, and E. C. G. for their assistance and support, and Paul Webb for compiling the first anthology of Bradford's poetry in 1988.

C. Caunter

From *Sonnets Songs & Ballads* (1908)

E. E. BRADFORD

The Child Divine

Methought I saw in visions of the night
  The Child Divine, concealed in mortal guise:
  His head was bare, no ray of heavenly light
  Crowned Him divine, but when His shining eyes
One moment met mine own, I saw them bright
  With more than human love: the starry skies,
  The world around, all faded from my sight,
  And I was lost in heavenly ecstasies!
Since then I seek Him. Here and there I find
  In one His smile, in one His tone of voice,
And in a third signs of His mighty mind;
  Then I look up, take courage, and rejoice.
But when in one I see revealed His Heart,
Him from my love nor death nor hell can part!

O Love, My Love

O Love, my Love, since time begun
  I think none ever loved as I!
Such love could spring from thee alone,
    With thee was born, with thee will die.
        The passion poets hymned of yore
          Seems worship of a vague ideal;
        None ever knew or dreamed before
          How sweet, how perfect was the real!

My love, O Love, none else but thou
  Could kindle, and 'tis thine alone;
Such love, O Love, is even now
  To all the world but as unknown.
        They love not thus who love not thee,
          One loves not so a vague ideal.
        The poets loved their dreams—I see
          How sweet, how perfect is the real!

"So as by Fire"

Sidney Swann, the motor-driver, when a lad of seventeen,
Went to Russia with his master, Count Dmitri Galitzin.
Wealthy was the Count, but lonely, wifeless, childless, weak
  and old,
Yet he toiled and laboured only to increase his piles of gold.

When he saw the wretched peasant selling all he had for
  drink,
Living only for the present, pausing not to plan or think,
Vast distilleries supplying all the country round he built,
Thinking if he throve by drunkards, theirs, not his, would be
  the guilt.

Thus he strived to shirk the blame, thus he kept his
  conscience quiet,
But at last his judgement came when the mob began to riot.
Swann was sent for constables. "Constables!" the sergeant
  said,
"All the constables in Russia could not give you help or aid!"

Now the huge distilleries flared and flamed with ruddy light.
When the lad returned, he said, "Sir, your only hope is
  flight!"
In the yard the sleek "Mercédès" glittered bright with
  polished brass.
"Flight?" the Count Dmitri answered, "they would never let
  me pass!"

Through the gateway, gently purring, came the motor
  gliding out,
Fast and faster, panting, whirring, soon it put the mob
  to rout.
Gleaming, as a flash of lightning gleams across a stormy
  cloud,
Rapidly it ripped its pathway through the angry, baffled
  crowd.

On and on to where the railway trailed across the snowy
  road,
Though the gates were shut it never paused, or turned aside,
  or slowed;
Like a thunderbolt it struck them, struck them till they
  tottered, waved,
Shuddered, trembled, burst asunder—and at last the Count
  was saved!

"Saved—so as by fire," he murmured. So in truth it proved
  to be.
Nearly all his wealth was plundered, but at length his soul
  was free.
He had lost his life and found it. Poor was he but not alone,
For his brave young motor-driver now was his adopted son!

The Mad Wolf

The boys came trooping forth from school: the brief, dark
   day was done,
One streak of red alone now showed the death-bed of
   the sun.
Off skated Boris and Ivàn beneath the starry dome;
Like a winding road the river ran down to their distant
   home.

For many a mile they sped full fast. Young Boris did his best,
But he was fain to cry at last, "Ivàn, I needs must rest!"
And as he spoke, the child looked back, and saw with mortal
   fear
A grisly wolf was on their track, and now 'twas drawing near!

Then Boris cried, "Ivàn, call out, and frighten him away!
It is but one, and if you shout, I've heard my father say,
The wolf will tremble when he hears, and turn his tail
   and flee—
Unless keen hunger makes him fierce, and that can
   hardly be."

The child was right. No veil of snow lay on the rich red earth,
The teeming forest seemed to show as yet no signs of dearth;
But gleaming eye and foam-flecked jaw has shown the
   elder lad
What soon the child with terror saw—the wolf was
   raving mad!

Down Boris fell. Then turned Ivàn to brave the frenzied foe.
A heavy stone was in his hand to strike at least one blow—
One blow—but one! The wolf came on with tusks laid bare
   for war,
The stone fell crashing through his skull—he sank to rise
   no more!

Thus often when some ghastly foe—some passion wild
   and fierce—
Pursues us as through life we go, we fly with cries and tears.
But turn, with faith for freedom fight, fling be it but
   one stone:
Thus David put his foe to flight, thus God will rout our own!

E. E. BRADFORD

Lines on Seeing a Child Bathing

The rising sun lights up his curly hair
  With just that same bright gold which gilds the skies;
The rosy dawn, which makes the clouds so fair,
  Flushes his glowing face. His deep, dark eyes,
Long-lashed, are shadowed like the sea that lies
  Beneath his feet, and of the same rich blue.
His slender, naked form the sunlight dyes
  With opal tinting of the very hue
  That shimmers on the foamy breakers too!

Some say man's beauty is but bait for love,
  As birds in breeding time wear plumage bright:
How can this be, when He who rules above,
  Still makes a child like this more fair to sight
Than any woman? Surely, 'tis by right
  Divine of innocence that children gain
Such spotless splendour. Standing in the light
  Of God's own face whence rays of glory rain,
  Like Nature, they reflect them without stain!

Paddy Maloy

O Paddy Maloy is a broth of a boy,
  As pretty as pretty can be;
He tosses his curls in disdain at the girls,
  For not one is so pretty as he.

Though he's seven years old, he's a bachelor bold,
  As for marrying, simply he *won't;*
His papa's in despair, for you see he's the heir,
  And the line will run out if he don't.

If a lady but touch him, his anger is such
  That he flushes as red as a rose;
But if he is kissed, in a moment his fist
  Goes simply straight bang at her nose!

What to do with a boy like young Paddy Maloy
  Is a problem to puzzle a sage;
I'm thinking, *ochone!* we must leave him alone,
  For it's too late to change at his age.

The Canon and the Chorister

't Was twilight when the chorister slipped shyly through
  the crowd
That streamed from the Cathedral while the organ pealed
  aloud.
He brushed aside the warm, damp locks that hung about
  his brow;
The cool air fanned his burning face. Well, it was over now!

He had not sung a solo in an anthem till that night,
And when he saw the crowded church, he trembled at
  the sight.
He knew his upper notes were good, and had a silv'ry ring,
But never dreamed so many would have come to hear
  him sing!

He went to tea that evening, still blushing like a rose,
With Uncle John, a Canon, who resided in the Close.
But though he had not far to go, he heard with cheeks
  aflame,
Time after time on strangers' lips, the sound of his
  own name!

When he returned, his mother said, "It's clear that all
  have heard
That John's to be our Bishop. What! He never breathed
  a word?"
"Our Uncle John the Bishop!" cried the youngster in
  surprise—
And all at once it seemed to him that scales fell from
  his eyes!

"Why, every one was full of it!" his mother rambled on,
"And yet he never told you! Well, that's just like
  Uncle John!"
"You see," Boy answered, with the frank simplicity
  of twelve,
"He had so much to say of *me*, and I—talked of myself!"

A French Boy

They think they are keeping
Their Baby Boy sleeping,
But night is now over, and daylight is peeping.
And Baby Boy long has been steadily creeping
Onward and on thro' the night!
Now the Dawn's growing bright,
      And the light
       Of plain Truth
     Is putting to flight
     All illusions of youth—
Those vague, phantomlike forms of the night.

My adorable mother
Has long tried to smother
All yearnings for knowledge in me and my brother:
When we asked her of *this* world she talked of the other,
Or kissed us and sent us to bed.
To the trash I have read
      I have said
      My *adieu*.
     I am not to be led
By old women, *messieurs*,
I will now learn of your lips instead!

I have heard to satiety
Maxims of piety,
Old commonplaces that pass in Society;
Truth would be really a charming variety—
Speak out, then, don't fear my surprise!
Come, open my eyes,
Make me wise
To know evil;
      Throw off all disguise,
      Show the beast and the devil—
      Tell the truth—I am weary of lies!

Reggie and Rover

Though Reggie's a laddie, and Rover's a dog,
   They are strangely alike in a way;—
They have similar hair—soft, silky, and fair—
And the same sort of eyes—grave, tender and wise,
That grow dewy in sorrow, and sparkle in play,
   And glow with devotion in love.

In summer they frolic all over the shore,
   And play in the water as well;
And one seems to remark in the laugh and the bark
A similar sound—full-throated and round—
Rather deep, yet as joyous and clear as a bell,
   And as sweet as the coo of a dove.

In winter they bask in the glow of the fire,
   The boy with his head on a stool,
And Doggie's quite close—his cold, wet little nose
Thrust confidingly in underneath the boy's chin,
And at night that's the way that they sleep as a rule,
   Boy under, and Doggie above.

They always seem perfectly happy. I think
   That love is the root of their bliss.
Boy's whole heart is set on delighting his pet,
And Doggie's one joy is to frolic with Boy.
And what is there on earth that is sweeter than this—
   Giving pleasure to one whom we love?

Mother's Boy

The children are weary of lessons and work,
  Now term's nearly over and holidays near.
They are always inventing excuses to shirk,
  And their governess feels rather huffy, I fear.
The elder girls suffer from "nerves"—well a day!
  I'm afraid it's the same with their poor little mum.
I know it sounds silly, but oh! I want Willie,
  I am counting the days until Willie comes home!

O Willie, my Willie, he's like a cool breeze,
  He braces us up as a whiff of sea air.
He's so thoughtful and helpful, and eager to please,
  We never feel weary when Willie is there.
His temper's so sunny, so steady and calm,
  He's so kind to his sisters and poor little mum.
I don't care if it's silly—I'm pining for Willie,
  And counting the days until Willie comes home.

"Our Jack"

Our Jack's a jolly fisherboy, a sturdy looking chap,
With stubby shocks of curly locks beneath his battered cap.
His face is tanned and ruddy, and his neck and throat
   are brown,
But his skin is like a lady's just a little lower down.
For he's always in the water, and is clean as clean can be,
And not a baby in the land has fairer skin than he.
There are folks, I know, who grumble and declare *all* boys
   are bad,
And when they see one stumble, croak, "A lad *will* be a lad!"
Of course, we know he will be, but I shouldn't be afraid
To back a lad that I know against any little maid!
For Jack's always on the water, when the rest are
   "on the spree,"
And the parson's little daughter's not more innocent
   than he.
Young Charlie's always ready to do his share of work,
And Freddie, when he's steady, is not the boy to shirk.
But when the lads get drinking—you may whistle for
   them then!
But you'll never find *our* laddie with a lot of drunken men.
For Jack, he keeps to water, or at most, a cup of tea,
And there's not a boy in England works more heartily
   than he!

Rain and Sunshine

Here by the sea, spring showers
  Fall harmless on the sand,
We need no shelt'ring bowers
  Where caves are close at hand.
     We greet the clouds with laughter
      They spend their rage in vain,
    The sun breaks out soon after.
     And a rainbow decks the rain.

But when my young friend, Teddy,
  This summer came to stay,
Alas! the rain was steady,
  It streamed day after day.
     The dripping quays looked dreary,
      Clouds darkened every place,
    Yet sunshine bright and cheery
     Still shone in Teddy's face!

Laughing late and early,
  At story-book or game,
He was never cross or surly
  From the moment that he came.
     And now he's gone to London
      I'd welcome streams of rain
    From sunrise until sundown
     If they'd bring him back again!

Boy Friends

When first I went to boarding school
  I thought the term would never end:
New boys *do* feel so as a rule,
  You know, until they have a friend.
       My friend was Jack—I found that when
        We walked to Berry Pomeroy; *
       And as I always think 'twas then
        I really first became a boy.

I'd never thought of foreign lands
  Until that memorable day,
But as we strolled along the sands
  And watched the vessels in the bay
       Jack told me where each ship was bound.
        Then as we crossed the sunny moor
       A lark rose singing from the ground—
        I'd never seen a lark before!

* A famous ruined castle near Paignton in S. Devon. *[Bradford's footnote]*

And when the castle came in view
  Whose fame had lured us from afar,
Jack showed me cells where witch and Jew
  Had shared the fate of thralls of war.
          He brought the pomp of chivalry
              Before my eyes; and by and by
          At dusk he pointed out to me
              Each star that glimmered in the sky.

And when at last in pensive mood
  Our sombre homeward way we trod,
Deep in the stillness of the wood
  He spoke of life and love and God.
          And now it always seems to me
              That walk to Berry Pomeroy
          Marks out just when I ceased to be
              A child, and first became a boy!

E. E. BRADFORD

From *Passing the Love of Women and Other Poems* (1913)

Fomes Peccati

A salt sea-breeze was sweeping in to land
  O'er sandy flats aflame with fiery heat:
But 'mid the shelving shore along the strand
  Ran out one weed-strewn rock that stooped to greet
  The boist'rous billows foaming at his feet,
Whereat his clammy coat of viscid wrack
  Grew soft and sleek 'neath their cool kisses sweet:
And where the waves welled up above his back
It showed all shifting shades—puce, purple, brown
  and black.

A bright-haired boy with beryl-coloured eyes
  Lay half-reclined thereon and half-afloat,
And as he felt the welcome waters rise,
  Soon sweeping swiftly up o'er breast and throat,
  Lifting his body lightly as a boat,
Then sinking till his slender naked form
  Lay bleak and bare, blithe as a wild bird's note
Rang out his happy laughter o'er the storm,
As now he bathed in spray, now basked in sunlight warm.

Close by his side a lusty lad lay prone,
  With brawny back, broad loins and swelling thighs
All dimpled o'er with muscle, thew and bone:
  His curly head half-raised was turned slantwise
  Propt on one arm, to let his thoughtful eyes
Drink in the radiant beauty of the boy
  Who, though his gaze was fixed upon the skies,
Perceived and thrilled with shy and modest joy—
The bliss of friendship pure—a bliss without alloy.

And I who passed, with well-approving eye
  In silence watched: then wending on my way
By chance I lighted in a cove near by
  On two young maidens merrily at play.
  Barefoot they paddled in a sheltered bay
Beneath a beetling cliff—a pleasant place
  Secure from prying eyes. One little fay,
The younger, had a sweetly serious face,
And all her slender form breathed purity and grace.

The elder child, she might be twelve or more,
  Was cast in coarser clay. Both seemed to be
The poorest of the poor: the rags they wore
  Could scarcely veil their nakedness: yet free
  As birds of air, and full of girlish glee
They chirped and chattered in shrill baby tones
  (Not noting or oblivious of me
Reclined at ease behind a heap of stones)
Rich in their youth, and gay as queens upon their thrones.

But when the sun sloped slowly tow'rd the West
  The boys whom I had seen before came by.
They stopped and stared. The timid child, distressed,
  Flushed as she caught the elder youth's dark eye
  Fixed on her own. The taller lass, less shy,
Leered at the lad; who, troubled in his turn,
  Blushed hotly; yet half-impudent, half-sly,
Strove with an air of manly unconcern
To meet her bold black eyes, that seemed to glow and burn.

25

And now the youth came closer to the child,
   Scanning her form with studied insolence:
Her sunny face, before so sweet and mild,
   Soon clouded o'er as shadowed by a sense
   Of something undefined. His gaze intense
Pierced through her rags, and where her tattered dress
   Yawned wide and left her breast without defence
He gloated on its beauty—none the less
Because he saw her shame and maidenly distress.

Had she been free, for sure she would have fled:
   She whispered to her mate, but all in vain:
The flaunting quean guffawed and tossed her head—
   Her wanton wiles soon made her purpose plain—
   To woo her wished-for wooer. Yet again
The dark youth drew a little nearer. Long
   He bent his eyes full on the child. Her pain
Was almost physical, when sweet and strong
Tolled out a deep church bell for daily evensong.

The lads looked on each other, shamed and shy,
   Then turned with mute consent to climb the hill;
And as I followed where the spire on high
   Pointed to Heaven through the twilight still,
   I pondered on that perfect life where will
Be neither sex nor marriage, and where Love,
   Having no carnal office to fulfil,
Will soar aloft on pinions of the dove,
Leaving his lower half, to seek his spouse above.

Love Laughs at Time

We met by chance
One windy day at Dover,
He young in years, I only young in heart.
He came from France,
And I was crossing over:
We met by chance,
And all too soon must part.
Tick-tock, tick-tock,
Cried out the cruel clock!

I scanned his face,
And loath to lose one minute,
Still strove to fix each feature on my brain:
Grasp all the grace
And budding beauty in it—
That peerless face
I ne'er might see again!
Ding-dong! the bell
Clanged out the quarter's knell.

But at the last,
In some mysterious fashion,
He laid his spirit bare—showed me the whole:
Then Fancy passed
With swiftly-passing passion,
For at the last
I saw and loved his soul!
Clock tick or chime,
Love laughs at fleeting time!

E. E. BRADFORD

The Bells Are Calling

Bells are calling, calling,
  Calling all to prayer:
Their mellow music mounts on high
  And trembles in the air.
They are calling, calling, calling:
  I can hear them everywhere!
Why then do I unheeding lie
  Deaf to their pleading sound?
O love, here is my melody,
  And here my holy ground!

Night is falling, falling,
  Falling from afar,
'Tis moaning in the mountain rill,
  And shining in the star:
It is falling, falling, falling,
  O'er all—save where we are!
But on this hill we linger still,
  Unconscious of the night,
For the radiance of love doth fill
  All heaven and earth with light!

Rudolf

Boys have no tongues to tell the love they feel:
  Yet one I know will stammer timid phrases
    When none can overhear:
And as each falt'ring word rings true as steel
  Nor woman's wit nor flatt'rer's fulsome praises
    To me are half so dear!

Boys' lips were never framed for eloquence:
  But one I know makes better use of his
    When none are near to spy!
Protesting speeches may be mere pretence:
  No words can say so much as one shy kiss,
    Nor half so prettily!

Leave women then to vow—and lie! not boys:
  But one of these—who's all the world to me!—
    When no one else is nigh,
Will clasp me round the neck: then all the joys
  His halting tongue could never tell break free
    In one long blissful sigh!

Eric

Implacable, unmerciful, fulfilled
  To overflowing with the sap of life,
      A male in ev'ry muscle, ev'ry vein:
Contemptuous of weakness, proud, self-willed,
  And cruel in his ardour for the strife
      That steels his heart to his and others' pain:

Impervious to sickly sentiment;
  Clear-headed though hot-blooded; logical,
      And fain to follow Reason to the end:
Careless of creeds and convenance, content
  To trample under foot conventions all
      So he can slay a foe or serve a friend:

Hard-hearted—yes! hard, but not heartless! Nay,
  Afire with love, pure, passionate intense,
      But love that knows no pity—fierce as hate!
He seems a child of that heroic day
  Ere yet man bowed beneath Experience,
      And followed fettered in the train of Fate!

Alan

Fresh from his bath, the boy, with hollowed hands,
   Luxuriating in the genial heat,
Before the glowing hearth a moment stands,
   Flushed with its rosy light from head to feet:
And thus I see him, naked, clean, and warm,
   Framed by the uncurtained casement close behind,
Placed in a picture lowering with storm,
   'Mid myriad snowflakes whirling in the wind.
His radiant face, illumined by the fire,
   Gleams out against a dark and troubled sea:
The shore, here dank with snow, there foul with mire,
   Lies all around his form yet leaves it free:
So is it with his heart—'mid shame and sin
   Unstained it glows with love's pure light within!

To Narcissus

You ne'er have met your mate as yet
  Among the maids who smirk and smile?
None seem to you both sweet and true?
  Well, you are wise to wait awhile:
For you are young, Narcissus; young
  And fair: far fairer than the few
Fair women foolish bards have sung:
  Then wherefore would you women woo?

You say they change. Indeed? 'Tis strange!
  What! cease to love you? That were vile!
But is it true they change, or you
  Grow weary of them in a while?
For you are young, Narcissus; young,
  I fancy somewhat fickle too!
But if your heart be lightly hung
  Say wherefore would you women woo?

It seems to me you're fancy-free;
  'Tis in yourself your trouble lies:
When you pursue a maid you view
  Your form reflected in her eyes!
But you are young, Narcissus; young,
  You still have time to start anew:
Let your own beauty now be sung—
  'Tis better to be wooed than woo!

Rondeau: Little Pleasures

When shared by twain, what seem but vain
And petty pleasures, forge a chain
   Of little links, that will extend
   And bind together friend and friend
As long as life and love remain.
For just as little drops of rain
Will melt and mix the parchéd plain,
   So little joys dry hearts will blend
When shared by twain.
And it may be, 'mid grief and pain,
The thought of them will come again,
   And Time a tender light will lend
   The pettiest pleasure in the end,
Once shared by twain!

E. E. BRADFORD

Ballade and Envoi: No Lover E'er Can See

No lover e'er can see
　With merely mortal eyes,
Whate'er his love may be
　He must idealize:
So when that Greek most wise
　First taught the commonweal,
Each saw in him arise
　His own ideal!

One wrote of him as free
　From human vanities,
A brief epitome
　Of high philosophies.
"Is this," the reader cries,
　As doubts across him steal,
"A God in human guise—
　Or an ideal?"

In him th' Athenian Bee
　Th' indulgent friend descries,
Who 'neath the platane tree
　With foolish Phædrus lies,
And toys with one not wise
　At Agathon's famed meal—
To thus immortalize
　His own ideal!

34

ENVOI

Prince, ev'ry lover's eyes
    Are blinded to the real,
And he for whom he sighs
    Is his ideal!

In the Dusk

Strangely sweet, and sweetly strange,
Chimes ring out, and die, and change:
And sweetly strange, and strangely sweet
Their echoes haunt the silent street.

Lying low in fire-lit gloom
The sick man hears them in his room;
All Heaven opes before his eyes,
He lifts his head, and smiles—and dies!

Basking by the glowing embers,
Stolen sweets the cat remembers;
Waking with a feline howl
He starts upon his nightly prowl.

Maidens meek, with modest looks,
Holding gilded prayer-books,
Cross the cold Cathedral square—
Where the young men stand and stare.

In the Minster vast and dim
Choristers commence a hymn—
Some who sing as sweet as birds
Note the notes but not the words!

In the "Dog and Bear" to-night
Men are "peeling" for a fight;
While the cheery chimes resound
Mates and backers gather round.

As for you and me, *mon cher,*
What we do is our affair—
Dusk will cover all until
Day shall dawn behind the hill!

E. E. BRADFORD

From *In Quest of Love and Other Poems* (1914)

In Quest of Love

I

Love have I sought, and Love I seek,
  Yea, and will seek until I die:
  I follow him afar or nigh,
Though I be halt and blind and weak.

Not woman's love that passeth by;
  Nor the world's love, so near akin;
  Nor love of that low self within,
More base than both: but throned on high,

Sexless, eternal, free from sin,
  Unvexed by passion, holy, mild,
  Pure, spiritual, undefiled,
Is that sweet love I yearn to win.

II

At first I fancied, as a boy,
  The Quest of Beauty was my care;
  To find a form divinely fair
Filled my young heart with fearful joy.

But Beauty delicate and rare
  Provoked an infinite desire
  Not for the flesh but spirit; fire
That shrivelled lust; a sweet despair

That filled my eyes with tears; and ire,
  Contempt and scorn for what was low;

And Love then seemed to me to grow
Far down amid the slough and mire.

III

I never knew the carnal sting
    That prompts to propagate the race;
    But as a youth I saw a face
Bright with the splendour of life's Spring

Where Love lay lurking under grace
    And turned my late despair to joy,
    Yet he was still too young or coy
To venture from his hiding-place.

My friend, a merry Irish boy,
    Made sport of all. In careless play
    We passed the livelong summer's day,
And Love seemed but an idle toy.

But once, as on the sands we lay,
    We kissed: and thereupon a flame
    Of passion pure that knows no shame
Showed Love full-grown. March passed to May

Without an April. Life became
    Like the rich rapture of a song
    That throbs with ecstasy. Not long
Could bliss like that endure. A name

Alone remains. First of the throng

That Love has lightened, first and last
  Love of my boyhood, he has passed
Beyond the reach of change or wrong.

IV

Sore loath to leave, I lingered late
  In boyhood's sunny paradise;
  And not till summoned twice or thrice
Passed I through manhood's narrow gate.

I found a world less scarred by vice
  Than by vulgarity. Low plains
  Where oft the Scarlet Woman reigns
Veiled as a nun. With judgment nice

She plays with moral problems—strains
  Out gnats and swallows camels. Sex
  Is all in all to her. She recks
Little enough of others' pains.

So sex-love be the cause th' effects
  Are justified thereby. Not all,
  Nay few are of this type; but small
In number, these can still perplex

The judgment of their sisters; call
  Good evil, evil good; and smirch
  The fame of manly love. The Church,
Austere of old, now seems to fall

Before these harpies; lets them perch
  High on her rafters, and defile
  With filthy droppings nave and aisle.
Whene'er in argument they lurch,

Evading the plain issue, guile
  Prompts them to turn to rhetoric
  To inflame the passions. Inly sick
With their rank poisons, for awhile

I halted in my quest. But quick
  Came Reason to my rescue. "See,
  The forms that Love assumes are three,"
She whispered. "One is gross and thick,

Yet comely still." She showed to me
  A lusty fellow called Desire.
  "The next," said she, "is made of fire.
His name is Fancy; winged and free

He flies 'twixt earth and heaven. Higher,
  Enthroned above sits Friendship. These
  Are worthy all in their degrees—
Three sons of one immortal sire.

But Lust, who loves himself to please
  Regardless who may suffer, springs
  From Hate, not Love. He bites and stings
And leads to death through foul disease.

V

In that old city, ever young,
  Where youth has for a thousand years
  Paid court to age, among my peers
I sought the love that David sung.

With hopes and fears I sought it. Fears
  And hopes were both fulfilled. 'Tis true
  A few I found, yet found I few

43

Who knew the love that brings no tears.

But this I found: that they who knew
  That love desired no other. None
  Can serve two lords. Yet many a one
Is known of her before the dew

Be dried up by the burning sun
  Of hot desire at noon; and these
  Respect and honour her. A breeze
From heaven, oft ere their day be done,

Cools them again, and by degrees
  As passion dies, the mystic light
  That lit their dawn returns at night.
Then e'en the married lover sees

Transfigured in its glory bright
  The loyal partner of his life
  No more as woman or as wife,
But friend and peer, arrayed in white.

VI

Love shone around me, like the bow
  That spanned the Flood, when staff in hand
  A pilgrim from my native land,
Twelve years I journeyed to and fro.

And Love illumed that Northern strand
  Where three brief years I made my home.
  No brighter shines the golden dome
Of Isaac's vast cathedral grand,

That like a star above the foam
  Of Finland's fretful waters gleams,
  Than shines the Love that haunts the dreams
Of mystic Slavs. Dark as the loam

That forms their virgin soil, and teems
  With riches inexhaustible,
  Their hearts volcanic, deep as hell,
Are treasuries from whence there streams

The crystal fount of Friendship. Fell
  Their wrath may blaze, and passionate
  Against injustice burns their hate,
But all who learn to love them well

Find underneath their fight with fate
  An ardour for humanity,
  A love in essence heavenly,
Selfless, sublime, immaculate.

This is no sexual passion; see
  Moujiks with flowing beards embrace,
  And in the public market-place
Exchange the kiss of charity.

See sober students gravely pace
  Arms round each other's shoulders twined,
  And mark, as mind appeals to mind,
How Love lights up each thoughtful face.

And see, once more, this ardour kind
  In symbol shown on Easter night,
  When kiss on kiss, and light on light,

Throbs through the darkness cold and blind.

VII

Through many a country far and near
  In quest of Love divine I strayed,
  And many a city where he stayed
My weary steps to me is dear.

First let my duteous hymn be paid
  To old Vienna ever young:
  Vienna oft by poets sung
And justly, for she is arrayed

In majesty. A crown is hung
  About her brows—a glorious ring
  Whose gems are palaces. No king
Has one so rich. Love, too, has flung

The light that Love alone can fling
  Like sunshine on her splendour. Still
  In memory I see it fill
Her meadow with eternal spring,

Where oft I wandered at his will
  With thoughtful youth or careless boy,
  And tasted the pathetic joy
Of fleeting Fancy. Dark and chill

Paris appeared by contrast. Coy
  Is pure love there: and yet there be
  Seven thousand who bow not the knee
To Baal's spouse, nor for a toy

Have bartered their virginity.
   Bound for the Promised Land above,
   Led by the pillared light of Love,
These cross unstained her foul Red Sea.

VIII

The Love divine has never ceased
   In poet-haunted Switzerland.
   With Death she wanders hand-in-hand
O'er mountain passes snowy-fleeced.

Her hardy sons well understand
   The love that triumphs o'er the grave,
   For they who daily danger brave
Seek the heroic and the grand.

In forest dark or mountain cave
   Their vows are plighted: friend to friend
   Is true and steadfast to the end
And gladly dies his mate to save.

Can I forget—nay, heaven forefend!—
   One sweet unearthly summer night
   I passed at Fribourg. Height to height
Is linked by bridges. Here there wend

All the day long—a wondrous sight—
   Both man and beast suspended high
   Across the gulfs, between the sky
And earth beneath. But when the light

Fades from the west, and far and nigh

The scene grows dim, each slender chain
　Hung between mountains o'er a plain,
Seems but a spider's thread. There I

From dusk to midnight walked with twain
　Whose hearts were touched with heavenly fire;
　And while they glowed with pure desire,
The words of Plato fell like rain

On thirsty soil. He could inspire,
　Even interpreted by me—
　As floods come though their channel be
Narrow or clogged with mud and mire—

A sense of the nobility
　Of that high love which lay till then
　Deep in the hearts of these young men
Unprized—as pearls lie in the sea.

It needs a pencil, not a pen
　To paint that scene. Each boyish face
　Lit with a new and tender grace:
The yawning chasm like a den

Of demon shadows trooped to chase
　Love from his throne: the trembling moon
　Now lit with hope as bright as noon
Now blank with fear: the lonely place

Gloomy with pines, and bleak in June
　As in December. Nay, no pen,
　No pencil do I need. As then
I see it still; 'twill fade not soon!

IX

It will not fade till life be done;
  It will not fade, but let it pass,
  For now in memory's magic glass
Another scene succeeds. The sun

Makes earth as iron, heaven as brass,
  Where underneath the cloudless sky
  Near Scheveningen there laughing lie
Two blithesome boys upon the grass

Hard by the beach. The sea-bird's cry
  Rings o'er their laughter as he wheels
  Close round their heads. All Nature feels
Love's madness. Winds are rising high;

The waving mill loud-whirring reels
  On every side, while wild with bliss
  The rosy children fight and kiss,
And louder still their laughter peals.

Two comrades met, but who is this
  Who walks between them as the third?
  'Tis I, I stole on them unheard,
Surprised their secret (which I wis

Was no great crime) and at a word
  Became their friend. For half the day
  Beside the dancing waves we lay
As careless as the wild sea-bird.

And then at eve, worn out with play,

Home to the Hague, in thoughtful mood,
We wandered through a shadowy wood,
Three friends together, I and they.

X

Scene follows scene now, thick and fast;
A sweetly melancholy chime
Of carillons recalls the time
I spent in Flanders. Hours I passed

By old canals, where, dark with slime,
The stagnant waters seemed asleep;
Or watching sluggish rivers creep
'Neath canopies of odorous lime,

While listening to those bells. The sheep
Cropt the lush grass, and drowsy kine
Peacefully chewed the cud. His line
Suspended o'er the embankment steep

Some youthful fisher would recline
At times beside me, and unfold
The story of his life, and hold
Me spell-bound for an hour. Divine

Became those moments when one told
Of noble aspirations, tales
Of heavenly hope that never fails
And heavenly Love that grows not old;

While heavy barges piled with bales
Of merchandise, or coal, or sand,

Crawled slowly by; and far the land
Seemed all alive with moving sails.

How hard it is to understand
  The secret workings of the heart!
  Love fills his galleries of art
In wayward fashion. 'Mid that band

Of Flemish boys, the greater part
  Strong, handsome, auburn-headed, tall,
  With clear blue eyes—above them all
I find one little figure start,

A child of twelve, frail-limbed and small,
  Pale, delicate, and nearly blind.
  He spoke to me in tones refined
In French of Paris, but withal

Swore like a trooper. Man in mind
  And cynical, he loved a jest
  So broad (as it must be confessed
Some Flemings do) that woman kind

Would blush to hear him. Gaily dressed,
  And spick-and-span from head to feet,
  He wildly rollicked down the street
Twisting a cane, that seemed possessed

With diabolic lust to beat
  Man, maid or child that came his way.
  At Brussels, on a holiday,
Up in the park we chanced to meet.

I know not how it was, a ray
  From Love, I think, enlightened me,
  But very soon I seemed to see
Beneath his chatter, shrewd and gay,

A lonely little heart. Set free
  The torrent of his love, so long
  Pent up, flowed tow'rd me, full and strong,
And when we parted suddenly

As we had met, amid the throng
  That filled the pleasure-loving city,
  My little comrade, bright and witty,
Haunted, and haunts me, like a song—

Some quaint, pathetic, old-world ditty
  Set to a brisk and lively air.
  I trow such cases are not rare—
Most of the gay deserve our pity!

XI

Next to our earthly paradise
  I turned—the home of joy and youth,
  In art the native land of truth,
In statesmanship of crafty lies:

The land that cut her wisdom tooth
  In babyhood, and still remains
  A babe in morals. Love there reigns
Triumphant, but has vanished ruth

And shares his throne with hate. Her stains
  Are manifold: her purity
  Translucent. Everywhere we see

Contrast, and losses balance gains.

Her glorious name is Italy.
　As for her sons 'tis hard to find
　A heart defended by a mind
Of ever-watchful subtlety.

I heard it beating low behind
　The lightning play of intellect;
　And often, when I little recked,
I touched it. Then by passion blind

Deprived of prudence to protect
　Its darker deeps, the boy would speak
　And show it bare. I found it weak
And womanish; its kindness flecked

By careless cruelty; of meek
　Subservient temper, but withal
　Proud, though with pride that feared a fall
And so walked warily. The sleek

Wild beast lay there: yet over all
　Reigned Love; and somewhere in the dark
　Enthroned sat Justice—touch her ark
And all that's sweet will turn to gall!

Beauty too common to remark
　Gleams everywhere—one form I see
　Whene'er I think of Italy.
A lovely youth who by our barque

Lay naked in the azure sea
　Before a score of ardent eyes
　That watched him gently sink and rise

In the Blue Grotto at Capri.

He seemed a fish of monstrous size
  With silvery skin of changeful hue,
  Like gleaming scales. His head was blue
And as he moved, the wondrous dyes

Chasing each other, charmed the view:
  The waters crossing breast and throat
  Flung over each an argent coat,
Which purpled as he rose. But few

Who gazed upon him from the boat
  Failed to perceive his loveliness.
  Protected by no veil of dress
Voluptuously he lay afloat,

For all to admire. No shy distress
  Disturbed his pleasure or his pride
  When men with one another vied
By double meanings to express

Veiled flatteries in an aside,
  While commenting effects of light.
  He heard, and understood aright,
And with his subtle smile replied.

XII

From Italy I turned to gay,
  Poor, proud, and pleasure-loving Spain.
  Once briefly viewed and not again
Ne'er will that vision fade away!

Warm-hearted, brave, and frankly vain,

Each boy you meet becomes your friend.
  If you'll but hear him to the end
He'll paint for you his portrait plain.

Prepared for all that fate may send,
  He takes her gifts without debate:
  Meets love with love, and hate with hate,
Prompt to accept, and prompt to spend.

Imperious and passionate
  In friendship, he will ne'er believe
  One is unwilling to receive
His proffered love. Why hesitate?

He wears his heart upon his sleeve,
  "Take it, or leave it, it is thine!"
  I took it gladly, made it mine
Without so much as "By your leave."

I well remember one—divine
  In beauty; child in faith; a man
  In love; vain as a girl: who can
Sketch such a creature in a line?

I see him flirting with his fan,
  Sat at my table in an inn.
  Our friendship neither did begin
Nor end, nor had it aim or plan,

But all at once the boy came in
  And sat by me. I made it plain
  That I was waiting for my train
That left at midnight. Could he win

My heart in twenty minutes? Vain

E. E. BRADFORD

Was introductory talk. He went
   Straight to the point—told how he spent
His daily life; what gave him pain,

What joy; where lay his natural bent;
   His friends and foes, alive and dead,
   And all they did, and all they said.
Believe me, twenty minutes spent

With such a boy sufficed to wed
   Our souls for ever! When I rose,
   I shook his hand—but he came close,
Kissed, and incontinently fled.

XIII

From Spain I travelled to her lords
   Of olden time—the mongrel race
   Around Tangier—knaves void of grace,
Moors, Arabs, Jews, barbaric hordes.

Despised and shunned in every place,
   These once proud peoples long have been
   Th' offscouring of the earth. 'Tis seen
Writ large in posture, form, and face.

The cringing ways, the servile mien,
   And shifty eyes, all brand them slaves:
   Yet there is something still that saves
Them from derision. In the sheen

Of Afric's sun 'mid sparkling waves
   Sport children delicately fair
   And nobly formed. With regal air
Old patriarchs, propt on their staves,

Wag hoary beards in chorus. There,
  Where beauty is, love follows soon.
  Alas! 'tis but a sorry boon—
Wild, savage, sensual, stript bare

Of all but primal instinct. Noon,
  Life's fierce meridian hour of fire,
  Flares with tempestuous desire—
'Tis oft burnt out ere comes the moon.

XIV

But pure-blood Arabs still aspire
  To nobler love. I think of one
  I saw last in the setting sun,
Walking, with feet that never tire,

Down from a mountain top. His gun
  Is on his shoulder: his dark eyes
  Keep watch to guard against surprise—
For foes grow bold when day is done.

'Twas in Algeria; at sunrise
  We started forth, this lad and I,
  To mount Beni Salàh. On high,
Far from the world and near the skies,

We drew together. By and by,
  As on the springy turf we lay,
  He told me in straightforward way
The story of his life. No sigh

Of sweet self-pity spoilt, no play
  Of fancy, no extraneous wit
  Relieved the solemn gloom of it.

While yet a child he met one day

A Frenchman, loved him, bit by bit
  Became, too, French in heart and mind.
  The Frenchman went, left him behind,
And th' darkness which had once been lit

By love alone, returned. Resigned
  To all, as Orientals are,
  He bowed to fate. But from afar
His eyes were turned on Europe. Blind

To sneer and scorn, the fret and jar
  Of uncongenial daily life
  Passed unregarded. Petty strife
Moved him no more; no taunt could mar

His inward calm; th' assassin's knife
  He would have welcomed gladly. All
  The sweets of life were turned to gall;
And pleasures of which youth is rife

Already had begun to pall
  On his still boyish palate. Grief
  So deep as this can gain relief
From nothing but the last dread call.

XV

Bright was my stay in Greece, though brief:
  The sunny hours were beads of blisses—
  Strung on a Grecian chaplet. This is
No rosary for prayer; its chief,

Nay only purpose no one misses

Who plays with it to pass the time!
And Love in that delightful clime
Is one long feast of fun and kisses.

How feebly can my halting rhyme
  Express the graceful gaiety
  Of bold Athenian boys! I see
Them still, and hear their laughter chime,

As gay, but never wild with glee,
  They gather in the theatre
  Just as the breeze begins to stir
The languid air. A spreading tree,

Broad branching plane or dusky fir,
  Serves us for roof. The lighted stage
  On which the strutting actors rage,
I hardly notice—round me purr

A hundred boys of every age
  From lisping child to manly youth.
  On sparkling eye and gleaming tooth
The lamplight flickers, while we wage

A war of amorous glances. Truth
  And courage light the clear dark eyes;
  The smiles that curve the lips are wise
With a tranquillity so smooth

That love's as calm as friendship. Cries,
  Loud laughter and broad jokes are rare,
  But fun and frolic everywhere.
I see one form before me rise

Clear from the rest—a tall boy, fair

As one of Pheidias' statues. Grace
  Conceals his strength; his glowing face
Is bright with health; his throat is bare

And in a softly-shaded place
  Beneath his open sailor vest
  Dimpled it sinks into the breast,
Just where the frail bones interlace.

The swelling bosom ne'er at rest,
  Heaves gently, like a windless sea;
  And as he shyly looks at me
His colour deepens, like the west

Behind the setting sun. Yet free
  From shame, because his love is pure,
  Sure of himself, and inly sure
Of Love's inherent purity,

He meets my glance with smiles demure;
  His happy, almost grateful eyes
  Showing without the least disguise
Pride that his beauty can allure.

Only the child, in playful wise,
  In Greece pretends to bashful shame:
  With him it is a merry game,
He has a thousand coquetries.

I see a boy with cheeks aflame,
  Upon a mountain top he stands
  Waving a pair of threat'ning hands—
A saucy rebel none can tame!

Up from the far Corinthian sands
  He guided me, on flying feet,
  To steep Acro-Corinthus. Sweet,
He drew me on with loving bands,

Caressing me. Then flying fleet,
  Dared me to chase him. On he flew—
  At times his form was lost to view,
Then he would wait. Scarce did we meet

Ere he was off again—I, too,
  In hot pursuit. But at the top
  At last the rascal deigned to stop
Defying me to kiss him. Who

Would not accept the challenge? Drop
  Upon your knees, proud captive! No!
  Down, as we came again we go.
From ledge to ledge I madly hop

Giddy and swaying to and fro,
  Until at last I reach the plain.
  Alas! my pains were all in vain—
I never kissed him, that I know!

XVI

In Turkish boys a love we see
  Obsequiously humble, nay
  E'en servile. Shall we therefore say
'Tis base? Base Love can never be.

The dog is servile in his way;

He cowers before the lifted stick;
  Cringes and whines if you but flick
His grovelling body. He will play

And fawn upon you, ay, and lick
  The hand chastising him. Yet slave
  To his own master, he is brave
To fight his fiercest foe. How quick

He springs to win the hero's grave,
  Giving his life for yours! Despise
  The servile! In our Maker's eyes
Are we not slaves? I humbly crave

With Paul that title: may I rise
  Through servitude to be His friend,
  But His, His bondslave to the end.
So I confess I highly prize

The love of Turkish boys—that blend
  Of gratitude and hope and fear,
  Meek, slavish as it may appear.
How often when I chanced to wend

Along the Golden Horn, anear
  The Outer Bridge I used to meet
  A beggar boy with naked feet,
Bare head and throat, yet gay of cheer

And clean though ragged. Up the street
  On seeing me he wildly raced,
  Caressed me, fondled me, embraced—
All for a few piastres. Sweet

Were his low tones; and as I paced

Gravely along, he cooed to me
  Dove-like. His ingenuity
In blandishments was great. He placed

His cheek on mine, he rubbed my knee,
  Tickled my throat, played with my hand—
  And all to make me understand
His impecuniosity!

"But is this love?" you ask. Not grand
  High or heroic love, I own.
  But ere you fling your dog a bone
He woos you so; and in that land

Beggars are dogs. The coin alone
  Could draw no love; but I maintain
  The boy—and dog—will woo to gain
The glance, the smile, the kindly tone.

XVII

When, after twelve long fruitful years,
  Again I trod my native shore,
  I saw not as in days of yore,
Nor blindly through a mist of tears

As often I had seen before
  My home in exile, but with eyes
  Lit with the light of other skies,
Keen with experience to bore

Through crust of custom, and to prize
  What once seemed common. This I found—
  The heart of England still was sound,
But not her head. Love never dies—

'Tis from the heart: but when not bound
  By chains of marriage 'tis ignored,
  And yields instead of peace a sword,
For love contends with love. Around

The flower-beds and velvet sward
  Of wedded happiness spring seeds
  Which often we condemn as weeds
Yet they are sown by Love the lord,

And not an enemy. Man needs
  Sincere affection; love he must:
  We satisfy a young man's lust
And leave his heart athirst. All creeds

Condemn this bargain as unjust,
  And yet the issue they perplex
  By making Love the slave of sex.
Would we our higher feelings trust,

Attend to cause and leave effects,
  We should not lean on laws and rules,
  Nor casuistry of learned fools,
Nor custom, that still vice protects.

Our Army, Navy, Public Schools
  Would show us love in boys and men
  High, honourable, chaste. The pen
Of poets would adorn it. Ghouls

Who batten now on slander, then
  Would glow with shame. But we defile
  The name of Love and make it vile
By hiring in a fetid den

Its venal substitute. We smile
  At vice that flaunts in every town,
  When we might fight and crush it down
By that high Love that blessed our isle

When Shakespeare sang. Though fools may frown
  That Love for ever shall endure,
  Romantic, passionate, and pure,
Life's glorious and immortal crown!

The Heat of Love

Some say the pure are cold;
   I know they're not:
My love is pure as gold,
   But oh! so warm.
If but his hand I hold
   I straight grow hot:
I burn if I enfold
   His glowing form.

Fire-red's his rosy face:
   But oh! his mouth—
It is the hottest place
   Beneath the sun!
His breath, when we embrace,
   Brings on a drouth
For kisses: in that case
   Ten seem as one!

What wonder this should be
   Since Love is fire,
For is not purity
   Love without leaven?
When Saints each other see
   With chaste desire,
Hell will be verily
   Less hot than heaven!

Shy Love

Little enough say I to Jim,
  Little enough says he,
Though now and again I look at him,
  And he at me:
But if by chance our glances meet—
My faith! I grow as red as beet!

Often I wait for Jim at school,
  Often he waits for me—
With the door between us, as a rule,
  I wait, and he.
When at last he ventures in the street—
Good gracious! how my heart does beat!

"Only a boy," they say of him:
  "Only a boy" is he?
Ay, the only boy in the world is Jim,
  At least for me.
And as for girls, I never meet
One that is fit to kiss his feet!

Heigh-Ho!

They say my gay young friend,
        Heigh-ho!
  Is caught by cruel Cupid!
Once hit his wit will end
        I know;
  Love makes a man so stupid!
When first the lad grew dull and sad
  My doubts were indigestion,
        Dumps, debt, or drink:
        Ne'er did I think
  That Cupid was in question!
        Heigh-ho!

Why *he* should be in pain,
        Heigh-ho!
  I'm curious to discover.
If *I* should sigh 'twere plain
        Why so—
  My friend's lost in the lover.
But if the lad himself has had
  No pleasure in his passion,
        Why did he fall
        In love at all?
  Just to be in the fashion?
        Heigh-ho!

His passion's fashion, ha?
                    Heigh-ho!
    If so, 'twill soon be over.
Well, *che sarà sarà;*
                    I know
        Young Love's a rabid rover!
Just now the lad seems very bad:
        Cure him I clearly can't.
                Then till at last
                Love's fever's past,
    I'll be his confidant!
                    Heigh-ho!

Childhood and Age

I

'Tis twilight, and the world is white with snow;
  My child is on my lap before the fire;
His sprightly little body all aglow
  With restless energy, seems to require
No aid from wordy eloquence to show
  His love unutterable; motion serves
To voice it dumbly; arms like tendrils grow,
  And slender silken legs in sinuous curves
Encircle mine, embracing them below.
  Nay, one adventurous foot to be more free
Has slipped its sheath, and now from heel to toe
  Vibrates within the hollow of my knee.
What intercourse could be so sweet as this
Where every motion is a kind of kiss?

II

'Tis otherwise with me; my body seems
  A torpid corpse, from whence the sentient soul,
Watchful and wide awake, already dreams
  Of taking flight. She now ne'er fills the whole,
But lurking in the brain, despatches streams
  Of electricity to divers parts,
Illuming them with brief, galvanic gleams.
  Yet when thus roused the drowsy body starts
To momentary life, it idly deems
  'Tis radical, and not derivative;
Nay, even now the warmth with which it steams
  Lent by the flames, persuades it it can live!

What wonder then it fondly fancies this
When my child-lover thrills it with a kiss?

III

But when my love, fatigued with amorous play,
   Falls back on speech, his soul peeps from his eyes
To beckon mine; reason resumes her sway,
   And lo! his little body gently dies.
My soul, no sluggard, hurries blithe and gay,
   To meet her sister with a wealth of love.
Then for a while we wave our forms away,
   Or rather leave them there, and soar above.
And though my love is young and I am grey,
   We hardly notice this, nor is there need,
Because a loving heart is young alway
   As soon as from the fleshly form 'tis freed:
And when our lips meet at a time like this
It is our souls and not our mouths that kiss!

First Love

Love now? Ah! No.
Love now to me might mean
  Man's cares too soon. You see
        This simple room?
        Its ceiling low
And white-washed walls have been
  My childhood's home—'twould be
        My childhood's tomb!

Nay, do not go,
But speak of sport or play;
  I shrink from themes above
        Boy's hopes and fears.
        Why need I know
Love's dangers ere my day?
  Tell me of life—leave love
        For later years.

And yet not so!
I feel that even now
  I am a child no more
        As in time past.
        Well, if wings grow,
And Love will teach me how,
  Maybe I'll learn to soar
        Aloft at last!

See! heaven's aglow,
The cocks are crowing—hark!
Ah! now the day is near
    Night's fear's forgot.
    Let childhood go,
I'll mount like yonder lark
  Where doubts are dead, and fear
      Remembered not.

Love now? But oh!
Where is the need for words?
  How can I help it—nay,
    Why should I try?
    If I could show
My heart! 'Tis like yon bird's—
  He's mad with love to-day,
      And so am I!

E. E. BRADFORD

Windows

I

I feel a sense of warmth and comfort creep
   Through every limb, as in my easy chair
   I bask before the fire. Beside me there
A dreamy boy reclines, and seems asleep;
Yet from his half-closed eyes I see him peep
   Through a far window. All without is fair
   With feathery snow; one path alone lies bare—
A little path across a warren steep
That skirts a wood, and wanders tow'rd the sea.
   The sea! It makes me shiver. Sweeter seems
   The fire by contrast—yet it brings me dreams
Of love, romance, adventure. Let them be,
   Disturbing visions! See the firelight gleams
If not like sunlight, bright enough for me.

II

Nay, there's no help for it; so soon I rise.
   The boy divines my thought; we seek the shore.
   The lonely coast is clamorous with the roar
Of foamy waves. How meek and wan it lies
In snowy shroud! The dreary daylight dies.
   Sad seems the sea till wintertide is o'er.
   As hand in hand we make for home once more,
The last faint glimmer fades from out the skies.
Then suddenly before us in the gloom
   Amid the trees we see another light—
   The Minster window radiantly bright
With Martyrs, Saints, and Angel forms that loom
Large through the mist, and call us! Nay, the tomb
   Is dark and chill: we will not go to-night.

III

Yet both those windows haunt us! By his bed,
  All robed in white, as free from earthly taint
  As virgin snow, my boy pure as a saint
Kneels meekly down in prayer with bended head.
I would not have him yet with love grow red
  Nor flush with shame. Let him dream on, and paint
  The future in fair colours, soft and faint,
Like Summer visions seen in Winter dead.
  And Heaven—that, too, can wait. Stay here awhile,
  But in your dreams see Saints and Angels smile
To make this life more sweet: and when 'tis gone
  Pass up at last where sins no more defile
Through that bright window whence high Heaven shone.

A Child's Delight

As I stand on the edge of a cliff
  Looking down at the sun on the sea,
There comes up a carriage; I hear
  The cry of a child mad with glee,
        "O mamma, look at that bird!"
And it suddenly seems just as if
  I were back in the past! Memory
Brings far and forgotten things near.
  What mysterious charm can there be
        In those few simple words I have heard?

I said them myself as a boy
  Just so, I remember it well,
Of a gull that I too had admired:
  I cried, as it mounted and fell,
        "O mamma, look at that bird!"
And I feel, as I watch it, the joy,
  The rapture of living, the spell
And the glamour of fancy that fired
  My innermost soul! None can tell
        What I've lost since I uttered that word!

What means this illusion of youth,
  This tremulous joy of the child,
This sense of the glory of things
  That is presently lost or defiled?
        Delicate, easily blurred,
A perception of Beauty and Truth,
  Though uncertain, and often beguiled,
In his spirit incessantly sings

With passionate pleasure and wild
   At the sight of a flower or a bird!

Is there anything later in life—
  This life—that can give us such bliss?
When a man is some fifty years old
  He knows well enough what life is:
      Sickened of hope long deferred,
And weary of purposeless strife,
  He may still not find life much amiss,
But he knows that the gilt is not gold,
  And he says, "Was it only for this
      That my soul, as a child, was so stirred?"

Scornfully comes the reply:
  "Never!" The visions I had
Were not of this world as we know it:
  Not of this world good or bad.
      Marvellous music I heard—
Wonderful, mystical, high:
  Holily, solemnly sad
As strains of a prophet or poet;
  Or joyfully frolicsome—mad,
      Ecstatic like songs of a bird!

I look at the fair little face
  Of the child: it is full of delight.
It will never be lit upon earth
  With a passionate pleasure so bright.
      "O mamma, look at that bird!"

He repeats: and I think when the grace
  And the glory of God, through the night
Of the death that is but a new birth
  First breaks on our wondering sight
    A similar cry will be heard!

To a Morose Puritan

If thou art blind, may not thy neighbour see?
　If thou art deaf, is he forbid to hear?
If thou art cold, must all men needs agree
　To banish Love, and harbour Doubt and Fear?
Say thou art straitened and thy lot is drear,
　Yet wherefore rail at our prosperity?
Say thou art sullen and of evil cheer,
　Yet why deem mirth and love impurity?
Our bliss is not thy bane; our ill would be
　No talisman thy clouded heaven to clear.
That thou alone canst do: I counsel thee
　To purchase Love, for though the cost be dear,
So to thy cost thou know'st, dear too is hate,
　And but one grain of love would change thy whole estate!

An Old Man's Dream

One summer Sunday afternoon,
The last in May or first in June
I think it was, I felt afire
With irresistible desire
To see my native town again.
'Twas but a little way by train,
I know not why I ne'er had gone,
But time had gradually slipt on,
And now full forty years had passed
Away since I had seen it last.
How weird that journey was! I seemed
As one who dreamed, and knew he dreamed.
All was so still as on we crept,
Each station looked as if it slept
In sanctified tranquillity.
But soon as I began to see
The landmarks of my youth, I grew
More dreamy still, yet restless too.
Here was the farm where once we stayed:
Along those river banks I played;
And now I noted, on my right,
The moor where we were lost one night.
That gabled house beside the pool
Was where I first was sent to school:
My bedroom window was the one
Now flashing brightly in the sun.
A whistle roused me; once again
It woke the echoes; then the train
Swept through a tunnel, and at last
Left me alone to face my past.
Outside the station, fresh and cold

The breeze blew as it blew of old:
And hills, and town, and beach, and sea
Were all just as they used to be.
The tide was low, long flats of sand
Ran out between the sea and land:
But now no nurse nor child was there;
The roads and gardens too were bare,
And all the country wore its dress
Of solemn Sabbath loneliness.
The parish church stood on the hill
Hoary with age, and calm and still,
But even as I looked the bell
Clanged out with its accustomed knell.
I entered: here again, 'twas strange,
I saw no slightest sign of change!
The window in the west was bright
With saints and kings who walked in light,
Their rainbow robes of gorgeous dyes
Illumined by the sunset skies.
The altar, exquisitely fair
With gleaming lights and flowers rare,
The delicately carven screen,
Flung like an airy veil between
This world and that beyond it—all
Remained untouched. I could but fall
Upon my knees, and like a boy
Pour out my prayers of love and joy.
Time had rolled back—nay, ceased to be:
Here brooded still Eternity.
The service o'er, while clear and loud
The organ pealed, I left the crowd,

81

And took my way high up the hill
Through a white, dusty road, as still
And peaceful as a country lane.
Now that the light began to wane
The silent villas all around
Waxed wan and ghostly. Not a sound
Was heard, save faint and far away
A steamer whistling in the bay,
Deep-toned, persistent: or again
The rumble of a distant train.
The setting sun had left a bright
Unearthly afterglow of light.
The moon was full; a fresh'ning breeze
Began to stir the rustling trees.
Here on the hill I still could find
No trace of change of any kind:
Each well-remembered house was there
And wore its old, familiar air.
The bright laburnums at the gate,
The seats where no one ever sate,
The paths where none e'er went or came,
The lonely lawns—all seemed the same.
But when the road came to the top
It did not pass the brow and drop,
As formerly, but led on still
Across another higher hill!
Amazed I stopped, then hurried on—
And now the dusty road was gone,
And I was on a grassy track
Beneath tall pine trees, gaunt and black.
The moon became so rarely bright
That the effulgence of her light
Turned night to day and made my way
As white as snow, or ocean spray.
Then in the glittering sheen, with joy

Close to my side I saw a boy—
My comrade forty years ago!
And straight I felt a youthful glow
Of life through every tingling vein.
No longer dreamy now, my brain
Grew nimble-witted; every sense
Keen and alert; and life intense
Thrilled all my nerves. "Arthur!" I cried,
"They told me years ago you died."
He lightly laughed. "They who are dead
Thus call the living. Nay," he said,
"Since I from living death have passed
To endless life, I live at last!"
"And are you still a boy?" Then he
Looked long and earnestly at me.
"I know not what to you I seem
For what you see is but a dream.
I am not man nor boy." He came
And kissed me on the lips. A flame
Like lightning, but more purely bright,
Enveloped me in blinding light.
What then I met I may not tell—
A Presence fair, ineffable,
Not seen, nor heard, nor felt, but known:
And when it passed I was alone.

.   .   .   .

I heard the humming of a bee
Close to my ear. Now I could see
'Twas crawling on my window pane
At home. It still was afternoon.
I have not met my friend again—
No matter: I shall see him soon.

83

From *Lays of Love and Life* (1916)

The Confidant

"Uncle, the King is dead!" cried Roger Grey.
"Long live the King!" Sir Roderick replied.
"So ends our Merry Monarch's joyous day,
And curfew tolls. Come, sit you by my side
And tell me all." Within the ingle wide
He drew the ruddy youth, and made him sit
Warm on the fireside settle. Eager-eyed,
Aglow with life, the stripling bit by bit
Emptied his sack of news, town-talk and tale and wit.

"Uncle, this morn my sprightly cousin Clare
Came down to play at bowls." A year had sped,
'Twas early Spring; out in the open air,
Snug in the old man's garden, by a bed
Of golden daffodils and tulips red
The gossips sat, high o'er the sunlit sea.
"Uncle, methinks if ever I should wed
Sweet Clare would be my fancy, none but she!"
The old man laughed, "Aha! A comely lass," quoth he.

Another year and more had come and gone,
'Twas Summertime, the friends together strolled
Along the shore, while Roger babbled on
Of rumours of the King. "And I am told
That Papist as he is, he grows more bold
To favour Catholics in every way.
And yet these rascals, bought with foreign gold,
Are traitors to their King and country!" "Nay,
Is't so?" the old man cried, "Alack and welladay!"

Thrice five revolving months brought Autumn round.
The old man and the boy walked through a wood
Of russet gold. "O uncle, I have found
Some Catholics are truly loyal and good.
A worthier man ne'er lived than Captain Hood!
He never means to marry, nor do I.
We walked alone yestreen in pensive mood,
And swore eternal friendship. Till we die
We'll serve our God and King, free from all human tie!"

Winter drew on. Deep in a muddy lane,
Sir Roderick and Roger, side by side,
In silence trudged till day began to wane.
Then in the deepening dusk of eventide
The boy said brusquely, "Clare is now the bride
Of Captain Hood. He married her to-day."
Sir Roderick said naught, but softly sighed.
And then he raised his eyes and looked away—
Prince William's ships of war filled all the bay!

Kings come and pass, and empires wax and wane;
Faith glows and fades, and creeds renew their form;
Light love takes wing; our bliss becomes our bane;
Youth's hopes are wrecked, and founder in the storm;
But ever true to its eternal norm,
Unmoved by restless passion's ebb and flow,
Sweet, sober Friendship, still sincere and warm,
Comforts and cheers us as through life we go,
Our stay in trial, our crown in joy, our balm in woe.

Joe and Jim

Are we the creatures of our age—
Mere puppets of a passing day?
Our conduct due to heritage
More than to will? 'Tis hard to say.

Two boys were born in seventeen eighty—
We'll call one Joe, the other Jim.
Joe, like the Age, was dull and weighty;
But Jim quick, restless, dark and slim.

Both boys lived in a seaport town:
No matter where. Joe was the son
Of a rich farmer—a mere clown
Who tippled when his work was done.

Jim's father was an officer,
Well-born, but poor for his position.
His mother—Jim took after her—
A beauty, and a great musician.

Both boys were sent to what was then
Described as an Academy
For youthful sons of gentlemen—
A trifle too pretentiously.

In fact it was a third-rate school,
Where boys were, by the Reverend Grey,
Ill-taught, ill-fed, and as a rule
Left to themselves for half the day.

Joe took to Jim: the stolid, simple,
Shy, rosy lad (then just eleven)
At praise from Jim would flush and dimple,
And feel raised to the seventh heaven.

Jim took to Joe: idealist
In love with tenderness and grace,
He had no power to resist
Joe's fresh, fair, flower-like little face.

As for the Age, Jim still was free
From its contaminating breath,
Its vulgar mediocrity,
Its soulless, humdrum life-in-death.

But then the boy had from his birth
A passion for the sea. His eyes
Were turned from sordid sights on earth
To bounding waves and open skies.

Again, the music of that time
No doubt had influenced his heart:
And this, most strangely, was sublime,
Soaring from Handel to Mozart.

Both boys now loved each other—both
Might well have followed one career;
Jim pleaded hard, but Joe was loath:
Does Joe's freewill at last appear?

Had he, or had he not the chance,
Which he would never have on land
Of soaring up to pure romance,
Love, honour—all that's great and grand?

'Twas on the last night of the half,
The two boys slept alone together:
Jim tried persuasion, coaxing, chaff:
Joe only listened to the weather.

The rain fell down in ceaseless streams,
The gusty wind shook all the house,
The lightning flashed in fitful gleams,
And Joe lay trembling like a mouse.

Surely he might have looked at Jim
When now and then the lightning shone?
If he had only glanced at him
But once, I know he would have gone.

For Jim was beautiful: his eyes
Were bright as stars with pure desire:
The love they showed without disguise
Could not but light an answering fire!

But Joe's were shut. He saw within
The creature comforts of his home:
He heard the thunder's awful din:
He made his choice—he would not come.

I have no heart to tell the story
Of Jim—it touches Joe no more.
He died with Nelson, crowned with glory.
But as for Joe our problem's o'er.

Joe had the one chance of his life
And missed it. Do you really care
To hear he married a rich wife,
Drank hard, grew stout, and died a mayor?

My Home

Alone at eve I love to stray,
  Pensive, neither sad nor gay,
As quietly the Summer's day
      Fades away.

From cottage homes fair children run,
  Greeting dad, whose work is done,
While mother brings the baby son:
      I have none.

In market towns old neighbours meet,
  Chatting in the shady street,
Where the air is cool and sweet:
      None I greet.

Through meadows rank with tufted grass,
  Winds a river, smooth as glass;
There strolls the lover with his lass:
      On I pass.

Here a hoary minster high
  Towers aloft into the sky:
The pious crowd pours in, but I
      Hurry by.

But when I reach the sounding sea
  Singing loud of liberty,
Where laughing lads are bathing—free
    Souls like me—

Here at last I cease to roam;
  Here beneath wide heaven's dome,
On the headland white with foam
    I am home!

Boyhood's Votaries

All worship Childhood's tender loveliness,
        And all can feel
The moving pathos of its meek appeal
        And soft caress.

Most men in Woman find the fair ideal:
        While some delight
In sober Manhood's wisdom, courage, might.
        But how few kneel

Before the little shrine of Boyhood bright!
        No marvel! These
Must serve a master often hard to please
        For wages slight—

A few shy looks and smiles: then, by degrees,
        Perhaps these rise
To shyer kisses: but no honey'd lies
        Or flatteries.

But they who bravely meet boys' candid eyes
        Self-knowledge learn:
Who taste the sweets of praise that they must earn,
        Mere alms despise.

And they who love green Boyhood, oft discern
        Before it end,
Hid in its sheath, the ripe eternal friend
        For whom they yearn.

In the Dark

By me, in the motor car,
  Sits a boy—a mere outsider—
Fellow visitor from far,
  For an hour my fellow rider.
      Dark's the night, no moon or star
        Shows his face. Thus flung together,
      English strangers as we are,
        Duly we discuss the weather.
  I hear his voice, I meet his mind,
  But to his body I am blind.

By and by a stray remark
  Touches me: I answer it.
Now what is he saying? Hark!
  That's his heart and not his wit.
      There it lies before me, stark
        Naked, bare, defenceless—mine!
      Love has hit it in the dark,
        Shot it with his shaft divine.
  Heart to heart, and mind to mind,
  Night's good as day since Love is blind!

Does Davie Tell the Truth?

Davie doesn't care for me,
    So he says.
Couldn't love me—no, not he!
    So he says.
But then he says it with a smile,
In such an enigmatic style,
I can't help wondering all the while
    Does Davie tell the truth?

If he loved, he'd love a lad,
    So he says.
Not a chap as old as dad,
    So he says.
But often after saying this,
He gives me just a little kiss:
So after all the question is
    Does Davie tell the truth?

Alexander Fergusson

Alexander Fergusson:
  Why, what a name it is!
A mouthful for a bigger one,
  I'll warrant you, than his;
For his is such a little one—
  About the size of this.
But though it *is* a little one
  It's big enough to kiss.

Alexander Fergusson
  Has a pair of eyes,
Brighter than the Summer sun,
  And bluer than the skies.
Say so, and asunder
  They will open with surprise:
But I wonder, *is* it wonder?—
  Or to let you see their size?

When I Went A-Walking

When I went a-walking
In the morning fair,
I met three boys a-running,
And one had golden hair:
Curly locks were they,
Like little rings of light.
I thought of him all day,
And I dreamed of him all night.

When I went a-walking
In the noonday glare,
I met three boys a-bathing
And the form of one was fair:
Snowy white, like may,
Yet rosy 'neath the white.
I thought of him all day,
And I dreamed of him all night.

When I went a-walking
In the evening air,
I saw three boys a-coming:
Two went I know not where.
But one went not away
For that I held him tight;
I'll work with him all day,
And dream of him all night.

Song: "When First I Fell in Love With You"

"When first I fell in love with you—"
"In love with me? In love with me?"
"A prettier boy I never knew,
And never wished to see!"
"But out with it! Come, out with it!
Never mind the first.
What of the present? Tell me true,
It is better to know the worst."

"Why, now you are big and brown and stout—"
"So I'm aware! So I'm aware!"
"A very good chap, I make no doubt—"
"That's neither here nor there.
But out with it! Come, out with it!
So since you saw me first
I've grown into a hulking lout?
Well, it's better to know the worst."

"Since first I fell in love with you,
And you with me, and you with me,
Of prettier boys I've seen a few,
And more I hope to see;
Still—" "Out with it! Come, out with it!
It's better to know the worst."
"I'm ten times more in love with you
Than ever I was at first!"

"Take It, Lad, or Leave It!"

Here's a loyal and a loving heart,
Take it, lad, or leave it.
Say the word before we part—
Take it, lad, or leave it.
Hoity toity! Where's the use
Of playing with me fast and loose?
Kiss—or kick me if you choose.
Take it, lad, or leave it!

All I have is freely yours,
Take it, lad, or leave it.
Love—or turn me out of doors!
Take it, lad, or leave it.
Shilly-shally, yes and no,
Won't win a friend or check a foe.
Hold my heart, or let it go—
Take it, lad, or leave it!

Cuthbert

When the sun is on the ripples in the West,
And the breeze blows keen from the sea,
And the fisherlad is waiting for the lass loved best,
Cuthbert comes for me:
Cuthbert, grave and severe;
Cuthbert, silent and shy;
With close-cropped hair, eyes dark and clear,
And forehead broad and high.

The fisherlad is welcome to his lass,
I had rather have my boy-friend far;
And I swim by his side through a sea like glass
Lit by Love's one star:
Cuthbert, ghostly and white;
Cuthbert, a bodiless soul;
Now like the Cherubim bright—
With a glorious head for the whole.

Tramps

I was tramping in the gloaming
When I met with Alec Grey—
Tramping in the gloaming
On a dark, damp day.
But though both of us were tired
And sodden and bemired,
From the moment of our meeting
We grew quite gay.
For each had found in other
One dearer than a brother,
And we laid us down together
In the soft, warm hay.
What's stormy weather,
And what's a little mire,
With a hayrick for a shelter,
And love for fire?

We have tramped it now a lifetime
Alec Grey and I—
Tramped it now a lifetime,
God knows why.
No end to it appears,
And we're getting on in years,
But still we keep on hoping,
And our hearts beat high:
For each has found in other
One dearer than a brother
And we'll lay us down together
When the end draws nigh.
What's a life of failure,
And what's a death of pain,
As long as we're together
When we wake again?

A Hobbledehoy

Do whatever you can
To a hobbledehoy
He will always be flighty and wild;
In passion a man,
In folly a boy,
In ignorance all but a child.

In love he's a fool—
Very often a knave,
As tricky and sly as a fox:
Now mad as a bull,
Now weak as a slave,
Now vain as the vainest of cocks.

When his passion's appeased
And his appetite faint
(For with him all's a matter of mood)
He is hard to be pleased,
A censorious saint,
A good deal too good for the good!

But in vain one abuses
His follies and sins,
And endeavours his faults to recall,
For whenever he chooses
Our hearts the rogue wins—
And mine goes the first of them all!

Love Purifies

There's no one in the whole wide world
More cleanly than a boy:
And yet who dabbles in the dirt
More recklessly than he?

There's no one in the whole wide world
In heart more pure and coy:
And yet who feels so little hurt
By gross obscenity?

Water washes off the mud
Till dirty hands grow clean;
And Love delivers flesh and blood
From every taint obscene.

E. E. BRADFORD

Youth and Maturity

Youth is the time for love, agree!—
   Nay, who can question this?—
And beauty too?—Ay, beauty equally:
   And yet there is
A certain splendour in maturity
Higher than fleeting youth's can ever be.

Youth is the time for love, for we
   Love what is beautiful?—
Partly, no doubt; and yet 'tis but partly,
   For as a rule
Lovers are all but blind, or they would see
The rarer beauty of maturity.

Youth is the time for love: youth's free,
   Love is creative. Youth
Appeals to Love by its plasticity:
   Its flaws, in truth,
Are baits for Love, whose holy task will be
To make it perfect in maturity.

Youth is the time for love; yet he
   Who loves, can love in age.
The older knight, long versed in chivalry,
   Best trains the page.
Sweet is the task, and sweeter love, the fee:
But sweetest Friendship—love's maturity.

Song: "Tramp, Tramp, Down the Street"

Tramp, tramp, down the street
Soldiers march with rhythmic beat;
And tramp, tramp come the pattering feet
Of the children around and behind them.

And a boy I love I shall see to-day—
And maybe see no more!—
Tramp proudly past and march away
To fight on a foreign shore.

Tramp, tramp, every day
Soldiers come and march away:
Tramp, tramp, brave and gay,
While the rattling drums and trumpets play:
Tramp, tramp—but who can say
Where we again shall find them?

To Boys Unknown

How often as I drift along the stream
Of city traffic, till the hive-like hum
Lulls me to sleep, and drowsily I dream
Of sweet days past, or sweeter days to come,
Some boy's fair face breaks on me like a gleam
Of rift-cloud sun, no sooner come than gone.
What if unhailed, unkissed he passes on?
Our hearts have spoken though our tongues were dumb.

How often as I ramble on the beach,
Where Nature seems asleep, and man is not,
And fairyland lurks all around, I reach
Some sweet, secluded, world-forsaken spot,
And startle there a shy boy bather. Each
Regards the other doubtful. Suddenly,
O'ermastered by some secret sympathy,
Each hails a friend, and doubts are all forgot.

These sweet encounters smack not of our earth:
These mystic boys, met once and never seen
In this life more, scarce seem of human birth.
Henceforth, illum'd by Fancy's golden sheen,
They haunt for ever poppied fields of mirth
Far from our workday world. The fairy Prince,
Mine for a honey'd hour, but vanished since,
Ranks with dream creatures that have never been.

The boys I know and love, though dearer far,
Have faults and failings. These fair friends unknown
Are Visions of Perfection. Naught can mar
The splendour of their memory. Alone
Immaculate, they stand before the bar
Of frowning Justice fearless. Sad-eyed Truth
Knows naught of them; and their immortal youth
No ravages of Time will ever own.

E. E. BRADFORD

My Love Is Like All Lovely Things

What is my love like? Why, all lovely things!
   I see them all in him. When he is gay
He's—let me think—he's like a lark that sings
   Soaring aloft to heaven: or let us say
      A splendid rainbow: or the clang of bells
      Waking the echoes in secluded dells:
He's like Spring, sunshine, flowers—all lovely things!

When he is sad, still all the loveliest things
   Bring back his face to me—he's like them all!
The woods in winter: lonely shores, where rings
   The Church-going bell, and evening shadows fall;
      Or moors in twilight; or a dying hymn
      Heard in an old Cathedral vast and dim:
The sea; the wind; the night—all lovely things!

Is this too vague—like all the loveliest things—
   You cannot picture him? No more could you
See what I see, without the light love flings,
   If you beheld him in the flesh. I, too,
      Saw little in his face at first. I thought
      'Twas fair, but stood alone. 'Twas love who taught
He whom I love was like all lovely things!

Old Friends and New

The boy I love is sweet and fair to see;
  One hour with him is worth a day with you!
For you, old friend, are mine eternally,
  While he is new.

One hour with him provides a hundred dreams;
  A day with you brings but a dream or two.
His lightest word a revelation seems—
  While he is new.

But well I know some morn I may awake,
  And find 'tis but a dream that I pursue.
You need not fear; never shall I forsake
  Old friends for new.

But if I gain his heart, your turn I serve;
  For all I have, old friend, I share with you.
And if I lose it, back to you I swerve
  With ardour new.

My Sweetheart

His mother made his body, Heaven his soul:
   And I? I did but teach his heart to beat!
And now his heart hath given me the whole,
   And he is mine—all mine from head to feet:
   All mine! And O my love, he is so sweet!

He loved his mother much, and Heaven more:
   And me? Nay, me he did not love at all.
But when I hit his heart and made it sore,
   He tossed it me, as one might toss a ball.
   And I? I caught it. Could I let it fall?

I caught it quick, and hid it in mine own:
   My beating heart soon taught his heart to beat.
And now I've not his wounded heart alone,
   But he is mine, all mine from head to feet:
   All mine! And O my love, he is so sweet!

Perfect Love

I pity those poor bards who peak and pine,
  Grow pale with passion, tremble when they sue,
  Shed tears, pass sleepless nights, and wail and whine
  To melt the cruel fair! I would they knew
Brave, wholesome, happy love like yours and mine.
  I do not weep, nor kneel and pray to you,
  Nor humbly venerate you as divine.
  Nor fear you—much: although I own 'tis true
When Love and Innocence together meet
  Love's held in awe, and so with me it is:
  But there's no torment in a fear like this,
It only serves to make my love more sweet.
For when I hardly dare to kiss your feet
  How proud am I to have your lips to kiss!

E. E. BRADFORD

Love's Magic

I tire of this, I tire of that,
And everything grows stale and flat
At times.
Art bores me, music seems to be
Nothing but noise, and poetry
Mere rhymes.
Only one of all my joys
Never cloys.

Often when the night is near
After a dreary day, I hear
A ring.
Then Art, and Verse, and Music too,
Revive as weary woodlands do
In Spring.
And when you come, my spirit's sun,
Winter's done.

A Little Child

A little child lay with me yesternight,
  If in the body or no I scarce could tell.
  His form was veiled in linen pure and white,
  Yet I divined its grace ineffable:
And though deep darkness hid him from my sight,
  Yet in my spirit I perceived him well;
  And when he kissed me, all the dark grew light
  And clear as noonday. Irresistible
Was his embrace, and as he held me tight
  And clung to me with ardour hot as hell
  Yet pure as heaven, I cried o'ermastered quite,
  "Can Love Divine in this slight body dwell?"
      Then knew I that this child of mortal clod
      Was but a blossom of the Love of God.

The Woodman's Boy

Deep in the forest beyond the town
I found the woodman's boy:
Ruddy was he, and tanned and brown,
Brimful of life and joy.
Saucy and bold as a woodland elf.
He has made me in love with the wood itself!
So it's hey for a life in the forest,
That is the life for me!
I want no wealth save youth and health
To roam in the forest free.

When I gave him a kiss he gave me twain,
He was neither sly nor shy.
His laugh was loud, and his speech was plain,
And he looked one straight in the eye.
I have done with maidens timid and pale;
He has made me in love with all things male.
So it's hey for a life in the forest,
Hard toil and manly joy!
I want no wife to smooth my life,
No friend but the woodman's boy.

From *The New Chivalry and Other Poems* (1918)

The Call

Eros is up and away, away!
Eros is up and away!
The son of Urania born of the sea,
The lover of lads and liberty.
Strong, self-controlled, erect and free,
He is marching along to-day!

He is calling aloud to the men, the men!
He is calling aloud to the men—
"Turn away from the wench, with her powder and paint,
And follow the Boy, who is fair as a saint:"
And the heart of the lover, long fevered and faint,
Beats bravely and boldly again.

He is whispering low to the boys, the boys!
He is whispering low to the boys—
"Turn away from the maids of the Evening Star:
My mirrors will show you are prettier far!"
And the rogues are beginning to reckon they are,
And are buying his mirrors for toys!

Aphrodite Pandemos beware, beware!
Aphrodite Pandemos beware!
Go get thee a tunic to cover thy throat,
Or ask Charity sweet for the loan of her coat:
Put a bit and a bridle, I pray, on thy goat,
And bind with a filet thy hair!

But Urania fair be glad, be glad!
Urania fair be glad!
The Goddess of Marriage has nothing to fear;
And to many a man, who would never draw near
Her fortified fane, is the Mother now dear
For the sake of her glorious Lad!

Boy-Love

I

Hard by a placid pool, where willow trees
  Half-veiled the sun, in marble majesty
Reclined a young Apollo: at his knees
  Stood a fair child of flesh and blood: to me
Fell Paris' choice. With heart and mind at ease
I gave the boy the apple. If you please

II

Crown the Greek God for perfect symmetry:
  This may appeal to old Praxiteles—
Not to an Englishman. A figure free
  From flaws at first can never by degrees
Progress in beauty. Immaturity
And weakness touch our innate chivalry.

III

Is Boy-Love Greek? Far off across the seas
  The warm desire of Southern men may be:
But passion freshened by a Northern breeze
  Gains in male vigour and in purity.
Our yearning tenderness for boys like these
Has more in it of Christ than Socrates.

Caw, Caw, Dreamily the Rook Goes

Caw, Caw, dreamily the rook goes,
 High above the high elm tree:
Deep in the dark wood, drowsily the brook flows
 Down, down, down to the sea.
O Willie, Willie, Willie, Summer holidays are coming,
 And I know that you are coming with the holidays, too;
The birds grow dumb; the brown bees hum
"Come along, come along, come along, come, come!
Every Summer comer's come again but you!"

Croak, Croak, cheerily the frog goes,
 Purring like a cat in the pool:
Each pet here, from the pony to the dog, knows
 Who's coming home from school!
O Willie, Willie, Willie, Summer holidays are coming,
 And I know that you are coming with the holidays, too!
And Love, little chum, beats a heart like a drum,
Rat-a-tat! rat-a-tat! rat-a-tat! tum! tum!
In a sort of merry devilish tattoo.

I Cannot Love My Love Alone

I

I cannot love my love alone,
  For although I love him best,
The passion that I pour on one
  Will overrun the rest!

II

And when my love is lately gone,
  The very air is sweet;
And half the rays that round him shone,
  Light every lad I meet.

III

Bright with his tender afterglow,
  The new boys at his school
Are troops of angels: those I know,
  Now wear an aureole.

IV

Rough lads appear no longer so,
  But changed I know not how;
Nor is there one so mean or low
  But he is noble now.

V

A little Lord, in sweet disguise,
  Kneels down to black my boots:
A mighty Duke (though small in size)
  Comes hawking Summer fruits.

VI

A Prince, in rugged raiment, cries
  The names of evening papers;
And several serve in humble wise
  As grocers' boys or drapers'.

VII

For all are Adam's family,
  My King is kin to all,
And they are boys, as well as he,
  Scarce tainted by the Fall.

VIII

With reverent humility
  I greet his courtiers;
My love for him, and his for me,
  Ennobles all his peers!

At the Fair

"Where are the whirligigs? Where are the whirligigs?"
Clamour a chorus of chattering curly-wigs.
  Where? They are everywhere—braying aloud!
Here is a fairing-stand covered with trifles, and
  Here you may shoot for superlative pots.
Crack! Crack! rattle the rifles and
  Bang! Bang! re-echo the shots.
  Eric and I are alone in the crowd.

Showmen who cry at us, roughs growing riotous,
Pushing and pulling us, serve but to quiet us.
  "Look at the moon, Eric, lighting the cloud!
Hark! Do you hear the sea?" Still as a nunnery,
  Peaceful and pure, are Love's sanctified spots.
Crack! Crack! goes on the gunnery,
  Bang! Bang! re-echo the shots,
  But Eric and I are alone in the crowd.

Piccadilly

Loitering in Piccadilly, looking at the shops,
What should I see but a vision of Apollo—
Just at the corner where Piccadilly stops,
   Passing into Piccadilly Circus.

Looking at a lithograph led up to a talk—
He says that *I* began, *I* say that *he* did!
Anyhow, presently we took a little walk—
   No one introduced us—nobody was needed.

Everybody praises Piccadilly shops:
Piccadilly picture-shops beat all the others hollow,
Especially the picture-shop where Piccadilly stops,
   Passing into Piccadilly Circus.

At Last!

Returning from Church on a fine June night,
With a shy little fellow called Merrivale White,
I was never so startled in all my life—
   The boy seemed altered quite!

Was it the magic of the woodland way,
The moon, or the scent of the new-mown hay?
I have no idea: but the fact remains—
   He seemed quite changed that day.

"Look here," he began, "you are going again,
And all this visit I've waited in vain.
Are we going to be chums? You know what I mean—
   Real mates? Put me out of my pain."

"But White," I demurred, "you seemed such a kid:
I like you of course, and I always did.
But all I can say is—if you liked me
   You kept it jolly well hid!"

"Did I?" said he. "Do you mean that you doubted
My feeling for you?" Then he frowned and pouted.
"Do you think that a boy can offer a man
   His love—and perhaps be scouted?"

"Do you think that a boy—and a shy boy too—
Finds it easy to come to a man like you,
And propose to be friends—real mates for life?
    You make a mistake if you do!"

"But I've done it at last." And there his voice broke;
And he lashed at the weeds with his stick as he spoke.
Then he went on fiercely, "Whatever you do,
    Don't treat what I say as a joke."

What *I* said or did doesn't matter a straw:
I could see there was no great need to jaw.
I suppose we behaved like a couple of fools—
    But nobody heard or saw.

I only know we were awfully late.
White's father and mother were quite in a state
Till the boy came out with a cock-and-bull tale
    That we couldn't unfasten a gate!

I shall never forget that night in June,
When the scent of the hay, or the gleam of the moon
Made a shy boy bold to break the ice—
    After all it was none too soon!

E. E. BRADFORD

The Kiss

I

He had never done it to Geoff, or to Guy,
  Nor to Arthur—not one of the three:
And I thought that he never would, he was so shy!
  But he did it—he did it to me!

II

We were out on the beach, and the tide was high,
  And the sun had set over the sea,
And the light was beginning to fade in the sky,
  When I said "You have never kissed me!"

III

I said it abruptly, I hardly knew why,
  But I said it impetuously;
For it seemed very hard to be bidding "good-bye"
  When my laddie had never kissed me!

IV

For a moment he flushed, and fell back with a sigh;
    For a moment he paused doubtfully;
For a moment I feared he was going to cry!
    For a moment I thought he would flee.

V

He had never done it to Geoff, or to Guy,
    Nor to Arthur—not one of the three:
But at last, as the day was beginning to die,
    He did it—he did it to me!

Too Deep for Words

The sun lay low in the Western skies,
    And gilded the Western sea.
"Eric," I said, "'tis a year and a day
    Since first you came to me.
I remember that time so well—do you?"
    "You bet I do!" said he,
"And the crab, and the beautiful Banbury buns
    That we had on the beach for tea!"

While a boy is a boy, he is far too wise
    To paint the pure lily,
Or gild refined gold. That day
    Was full of poetry.
That could never be put into word he knew:
    Can the highest ever be?
And surface sentimental talk
    Seemed sheer profanity.

So he just looked up with the love-lit eyes
    That he seldom lets me see,
And then, as I pressed the hand that lay
    In mine confidingly,
With a shy little laugh, and a bright flush too,
    "You bet I do!" said he,
"And the crab, and the beautiful Banbury buns
    That we had on the beach for tea!"

Hilary

I

Hilary is seventeen;
  Hopeful, though his home's an attic;
Optimistic and serene,
  Though his future's problematic:
        Hopeful as to what has been,
          Hopeful as to what's to be, too:
        What remains still to be seen
          Is—is there any hope for me, too?

II

Hilary's inclined to lean
  To a love so democratic,
It embraces the most mean,
  Most repulsive, most erratic!
        Full of love is he I ween—
          So all say, and so I see, too:
        What remains still to be seen
          Is—has he love to spare for me, too?

Frank

I

What led him to lay
  His whole heart bare,
When nothing compelled him to?
  Looking away
With a vacant stare,
He dragged all out to view!

II

There lay a frail
  Bark, launched on life,
At grips with beast and devil:
  Now his artless tale
Would cut like a knife,
Now dance in a witches' revel!

III

Talk of a fair
  Unveiling her form
To a lover!—What's that to this?
  This boy laid bare
His soul to the storm—
Not his skin to a lover's kiss.

IV

Well, he has his reward;
  He has won his prize;
(What he sought—be it rich or poor!)
  Truth touched the chord—
And my heart replies,
And will echo till life be o'er!

I Saw Will Home One Windy Night

I

I saw Will home one windy night.
  (O how the blast did blow!)
I held his hand, and gripped it tight,
  The storm was raging so.
The ground was white
  With driven snow,
But Love can warm like wine,
  And heat and light
  Both seemed to flow
From the hand I held in mine!

II

Ere he was home, Will tripped and fell.
  (O how my heart did beat!)
His ankle, sprained, began to swell,
  And the wind grew wet with sleet.
A burden sweet,
  O'er hill and dell,
I bore him after this:
  But aching feet
  And arms grew well
When he paid me with a kiss!

May Flowers

Deep in a sheltered nook; mid hawthorn trees
Laden with snowy blossoms, on the grass,
A lusty ploughboy flung himself at ease,
Close to a pool, whose waters seemed of glass.
As, one by one, his russet rags he doffed,
And let them drop like dead leaves to the earth,
He showed a glowing form, as fair and soft
As is the tender infant's at its birth:
And when, at length, he stood in naked pride,
A boy in beauty, but a man in might,
He put to shame the blossoms at his side,
As sanguine Dawn blots out anæmic Night;
    No other bloom seemed half so sweet and fresh
    As this majestic flower of the flesh!

Corpus Sanum

'Tis sweet to toil when youth makes labour light,
'Tis sweet to eat with healthy appetite,
'Tis sweet to sleep in dreamless ease at night,
                    Tired through and through.

'Tis sweet to learn, with secret shy delight,
That day by day with manhood's growing might
Comes greater power to love, new visions bright,
                    And day dreams new.

Youth's tender body, clean and rosy-white,
Is not that flesh corrupt we have to fight:
Its natural appetites are sane and right;
                    Its instinct true.

The mere word "carnal" shall not me affright;
Nor will I cease, in Puritans' despite,
To love the boyish body with the sprite,
                    And hymn it too.

The Purity of Youth

A boy makes no parade of holiness,
  But hides it in his soul's most secret place:
But lest the careless eye should pass it by,
  God writes it plainly on his radiant face.

His tongue will rarely utter his distress,
  Keen though it be, at what is foul or base:
God therefore shows his shy, sweet purity
  In all his slender form's unearthly grace.

Love him, and you will learn his heavenly dress
  Is sacramental: but in any case
E'en if his form should lie, his modesty
  Would linger in his kiss and his embrace.

Youth and Age

I

Doth God make Youth
    At first
    So beautiful,
Knowing his need
    To harden
    And mature—
That while uncouth,
    Unversed,
    Undutiful,
His form may plead
    For pardon
    And allure?

II

Age He endueth
    With meet
    Serenity,
Gentle to sin,
    Being of
    Himself secure;
Combining truth
    With sweet
    Amenity,
That he may win
    Youth's love
And keep him pure.

III

The faults of Youth,
     And his
       Bare beauty too,
Are quickly done;
     But both,
       While they endure,
Give Age in sooth
     A bliss
       And duty too,
To love the one,
     Nor loathe
The rest, but cure.

E. E. BRADFORD

The Bather in the Blue Grotto at Capri

Prepared to dive, he flings aside his vest,
And waits the signal. Brown's his curly hair,
Deep brown his eyes, and now we see it bare,
Though face and hands are browner than the rest,
Save two brown nipples on his boyish breast,
His sun-burnt body's nut brown everywhere.
He stands a moment, lit up by the glare
Of light reflected, grave and self-possessed.
Then down he drops deep in the deep-blue wave,
And re-appears a merman. Silvery scales
Gleam on the grey-blue skin that covers him.
Henceforth he is a creature of the cave—
A fish with human head, and two long tails;
A mythologic monster, sleek and slim.

The Stolen Visit

Two light feet,
With a rhythmic beat,
Are galloping along in a lonely street.

Two friends meet
In a storm of sleet—
Their heaven upon earth is a garden seat.

Two hearts sweet,
For a moment fleet,
Are throbbing in accord with love replete.

Two light feet,
In a swift retreat,
Are galloping away in a lamp-lit street.

On Sunday Night

I

I saw Chris off on Sunday night,
  Thus missing evensong.
Chris hardly thought that this was right;
  But right or wrong,
When I proposed it, he was so delighted
That very soon his sense of wrong was righted.

II

It seemed at first as if the clang
  Of bells would never cease;
But when the chimes no longer rang,
  The ensuing peace
Was so profound that our disturbing feet
Woke angry echoes all along the street.

III

Here at a casement window sat,
  With Bible open wide,
A prim old lady, while her cat
  Purred at her side:
Both looked at us with disapproval. Chris
Was greatly discomposed on noting this.

IV

Some sinners lounging in the square,
  Outside the silent inn,
Gave us a long enquiring stare.
  Then with a grin
Made *sotto voce* comments—to the effect
That we were fellow sinners I suspect.

V

Chris looked uncomfortable. Yet
  I somehow think, at heart
He rather liked it, for it set
  Us two apart,
Branded with the romantic mark of Cain,
Outlaws from realms where peace and order reign.

VI

He whistled recklessly a tune
  That first was like a hymn,
Sober and slow, but very soon
  It bore a dim
Resemblance to a well-known comic song
But this bravado did not last for long,

VII

For as we climbed the sunny hill,
　　Crowned with a shadowy wood,
All seemed so solemn and so still
　　That he grew good,
And sung a psalm, with all its proper words,
Rousing a chorus of responsive birds.

VIII

Then growing tired, we lay at rest,
　　Half hid by branching bracken,
And watched the sun sink in the West,
　　And saw the tree trunks blacken
Against the saffron sky. Then, with his head
Pillowed upon my lap, as if in bed,

IX

Chris told me secrets—hopes and fears
　　His troubles and his joys;
The men he liked among my peers,
　　And favourite boys,
But added shyly after this review,
"But there's not one I love so much as you."

X

We rose, and through the darkening wood
  Pursued our onward way:
Then suddenly, in pensive mood
  Chris stopped to say
Impressively, "Just think! It's Sunday night!
How odd it seems! I can't believe it quite.

XI

"What's father doing now? *You* guess.
  I say he's reading prayers.
Or is he preaching?" Some distress
  Came unawares
Into his voice, as he went on "While we
Seem as un-Sundayfied as we can be!"

XII

But now the trees were growing rare;
  In groups of three or four
They formed a fringe upon a bare,
  Heath-covered moor.
Through this we plodded somewhat wearily,
While distant engines whistled eerily.

XIII

Then, as the night began to fall,
  And we could see at last
The lighted railway-station, all
  His good fit past,
Chris grew excited at the moving lights,
The screaming whistles, and the un-Sunday sights.

XIV

"Come on!" His feet began to dance,
  He ruffled up his hair,
'Twas plain that virtue had no chance—
  The noise, the glare,
The bustle and confusion of the crowd,
Were all too much for him. He laughed aloud.

XV

But when his train came down the line,
  His face grew white,
He slipped one little hand in mine,
  And gripped it tight:
The thought of parting cut him like a knife,
He felt the awful tragedy of life.

XVI

And I? I might have had more sense,
   And yet at heart I knew
There was but little difference
   Between us two!
It was but being a bigger hypocrite
I'd learnt to feel without betraying it!

XVII

"Goodbye!" I meant to shake his hand,
   And go, but to my joy,
Such ways Chris could not understand.
   I think the boy
Saw no one's eyes upon him but my own,
And kissed me just as if we were alone.

XVIII

A whistle, and the train was off,
   Lost in the misty air:
And then I heard an old man cough,
   Some sailors swear,
A baby wail. How dull this world would be
Without youth's sweet romance and poetry!

Love's Labour Lost

I

At times I deem love's labour lost:
　By giving beings breath,
We multiply but at the cost
　Of multiplying death!

II

While woman bears, with travail pain,
　The everlasting soul;
And Death delivers it again,
　What gain we on the whole?

III

I have no heart to procreate
　Earth-children for the sword:
The Love that links me to my mate,
　Himself is his reward.

From *The Romance of Youth and Other Poems* (1920)

The Romance of Youth

"He whom the gods love dearly dies in youth".
So sang the poet in the pagan past:
So, in a sort, dies every boy in sooth;
Romantic, ardent, joyous to the last,
He runs to welcome Death, who holds him fast;
And even as we gaze the Boy is gone,
The virile toga round his form is cast,
And "not unclothed" by Death "but clothed upon"
Into a larger life he swiftly passes on.

The Boy is dead: the Man is not the Boy
Save as the disembodied Saint is Man.
Behold his eyes have lost the light of joy;
The naked feet on which to Death he ran,
Are booted with the buskins of grave plan
Or socks of dalliance. His curls, confined
By cap or crown, no careless breeze can fan,
Nor loving finger fondle. Calm, resigned,
He marches tow'rd the night, and leaves the dawn behind.

Yet Childhood's dawn is part of Nature's plan:
The Boy's the treble of her harmony.
He understands her secrets more than Man,
And serves as link with bird and beast and tree.
His heart beats closer to the mystery
Of Universal Being, and his eyes
Perceive a Light that ours no longer see—
A light that lingers in the sunset skies,
Gleams faintly in the stars, and never wholly dies.

For though the boy may pass, the Boy Ideal
Will live for ever. In the hero's soul
He reigns supreme, and Saints and Sages kneel
Before his throne, for Nature's perfect whole
Is not entire without him. Fawn and foal,
Shrill-bleating lamb, all beings fair and small,
Shy woodland creatures—squirrel, stoat and mole,
Invisible birds that in the twilight call—
All share his sweet romance, but he transcends them all.

The Boy reigned in Judaea as her King,
Her Saint, her Bard, her Prophet. 'Tis a Boy
Who never ceases in her psalms to sing
His Heavenly Father's care. His harp's a toy,
And to the end he is a child—the same
As he who eyed his friend, reserved and coy,
But gravely happy, both his cheeks aflame
With that all-glorious love that leaves no after shame.

He reigned in Greece: it was a wayward Boy,
But lovable, and pure, and twice as fair
As man can ever be, who sulked at Troy,
Nursing a petty feud—too young to bear
His weight of glory and his people's care.
But by good hap a faithful friend and strong,
Yet tender as a mother mild was there,
Who dying in his stead, drew him along
With silken cords of love to join the immortal throng.

Reigned he in Rome? One melancholy youth
Reigned in the heart of him who reigned o'er all:
But was the fair Bithynian Boy in truth
The idol of the Romans? I recall
No love like David's for the son of Saul;
But low intrigues with slaves and pampered pages,
And frolicking with freedom—what a fall
From that pure passion sanctioned by her sages
And handed down by Greece to all succeeding ages!

In Britain boys are friendless: happy they
Whose youth is spent in shadow: for the few
Whom Birth or Genius lightens with a ray
Of early fame, grow dazzled, and pursue
Their aftercourse at hazard, as steeds do
Alarmed and riderless: and many a one
For lack of a protector kind and true,
Has died in youth; as David might have done,
Had not his heartless king a kinder-hearted son.

Behold yon gallant youth with golden hair
That streams behind him like a comet's tail,
Who gallops gaily on a courser fair
To beard a scowling mob. A trifle pale,
But calm and confident, the stripling frail
Essays alone to win the rebel crowd.
His courtiers stand in doubt. Will youth prevail?
One breathless moment all the host is cowed,
Then Man acclaims the boy with plaudits long and loud.

O that a friend with virile heart and brain
Had loved him ere that glorious day was done,
Caressed and cockered him, in prophet strain,
Dubbed him the great Black Prince's genial son,
Yet while well-pleased with what was well begun,
Suggested greater consequents, and so
By hortatory adulation won
The wayward will to virtue! But the glow
Of generous fire flared out, and died in ashes low.

Arthur of Brittany—the little ghost
That hovers round King John—the luckless twain
King Edward and young York, as wan almost
As their white roses, sought and sought in vain
A single faithful friend: and once again
We meet a boy King Edward, friendless too,
When fatherless he entered on his reign:
Pale patron saint of the pale scholar crew
He knew and shared their toil, their prize he never knew.

And they whom Genius lightened fared as ill.
There was a boy whom all men marvelled at
But none befriended. In a parvis still
At eve alone with lean Church mouse and rat,
Watched by the blinking owl and wheeling bat,
He penned his wondrous poems, till he passed
Into a city attic, where he sat
More lonely still, in solitude more vast,
Until he found in Death one kindly friend at last.

And Adonais, had he met a mate—
Some young Endymion or Calidore—
Might not he too have triumphed over fate
And kept the crown he won but never wore?
But when he wandered on the Devon shore,
Or sauntered sadly o'er the Scottish heath,
A lonely exile sick at heart and sore,
He tells us almost with his latest breath
He was already "half in love with easeful Death."

It is not good the Boy should be alone:
He needs an helpmeet even more than man.
Yet if the brethren of his flesh and bone
Are framed and fashioned on a diverse plan,
A Joseph, or a lion's whelp like Dan
Destined to leap from Bashan, lives apart
Most homeless when at home. None will or can
Light up the dark recesses of his heart,
Bind up his spirit's wounds, or mollify their smart.

Most lonely at the festival of love,
He pines amid uproarious jollity:
The frosty stars in the chill vault above
Are not more far removed from mirth than he!
While rhythmic music, dance, and cries of glee
Throb round him in the lighted drawing-room,
He sadly eyes the tempest-shaken tree
That seems to beckon to him from the gloom.
What should be home to him's a prison or a tomb!

Could he but steal away and be at rest
With mother Nature and one favourite friend,
Pillow his head on some responsive breast,
Lay bare his heart, and let his Mentor blend
Sweet comfort with wise counsel at the end,
How often would the boyish Ishmaelite,
The stubborn rebel, the child Cain unbend:
For he who braves the boisterous wind's rude might,
Will cast away his cloak when once the sun shines bright.

He cannot plead for love—his heart's in trance,
A Sleeping Beauty. Surely he has no need?
His innocence, his halo of romance,
His boyish bloom, his very dumbness plead!
Is there no knight from lower passion freed
To succour him who has no power to call,
And can requite his service with no meed?
Is there no Galahad or Parsifal,
Who finds in heavenly love the highest bliss of all?

Love of the heart alone—Love all romance,
All tenderness, all purity and light,
Will wake the Sleeping Beauty from his trance,
Ennoble him, and glorify his Knight:
And when the world has seen this vision bright,
All Love will be transfigured, for the boy
So crowned in youth, and early robed in white,
Will look at woman with a purer eye,
And seek from her, in turn, the Love that cannot die.

Poetry

From earliest childhood have I seen at times
   A fleeting Beauty, exquisite and rare.
But when I strove to fix it in my rhymes,
   No other eye than mine could see it there:
   The life had gone, the words lay cold and bare.

This radiance, delicate and fugitive,
   Is not mere loveliness of form and line;
But more like sunlight, which has power to give
   A grace to all on which it deigns to shine,
   Gilding the meanest things with gold divine.

It comes and goes as swiftly: now and then
   It glorifies a little group of trees,
A lonely road, a lake, a twilight glen:
   It sweeps across them, like a passing breeze,
   Displaying more than mortal eye e'er sees.

I find it most in savage Nature: still
   'Tis only latent in her. I may gaze
Long hours unmoved at sea and plain and hill,
   Then suddenly it shimmers thro' a haze,
   And passes rapidly from phase to phase.

It lights my spirit rather than my eyes,
  Suggesting more than I can ever see:
Sometimes, I think, awaking memories
  As Plato taught: sometimes it seems to me
  Like a foretaste of bliss about to be.

And afterwards I feel as one who wakes
  Reluctant from a dream, and strives in vain
To dream once more, and for this purpose makes
  A recapitulation, bare and plain,
  Of what he saw, and hopes to see again.

Of this I am resolved—I will not smear
  My canvas with excess of gaudy paint,
But keep at least the outline firm and clear;
  And if the colouring be cold and faint,
  No matter so 'tis free from earthly taint.

Truth

I will not weave of lovely lies
   A wimple veil to shield my soul,
But rather with unhooded eyes
   Face naked Truth and see her whole.

I will not drift in idle dreams
   On moonlight meres of poppied bliss,
But rather from the world that seems
   I will awake to that which is—

The glorious world of wold and wood,
   The world of blithesome birds and boys,
The world that whispers "God is good,
   And takes delight in all our joys!"

Boyhood

Boyhood I worship rather than the boy;
  And boyhood but as part of Nature's whole,
Her fairest blossom, telling of her joy
  Her hope her love; the tongue whereby her soul,
Imprisoned in the brute, still hardly freed,
  Not wholly dumb nor quite articulate,
Not warped by prejudice nor cramped by creed,
  Babbles of deepest mysteries of fate.
And if awhile I worship one alone,
  That one to me is Nature, and a vision,
Though blurred, of Him Who sits upon her throne,
  And sheds His glory on the fields Elysian.
But boy, as boy, is not so inly dear
As man, my fellow-worshipper and peer.

A Starry Night

Wild winds of March are piping shrill
  In wold and wooded alley,
They bow the birches on the hill,
  And the willows in the valley.

But through a lace-like tracery
  Of branches dark and slender,
There gleams a starry canopy
  Of palpitating splendour:

The Greater and the Lesser Bear,
  The Dragon and the Lion,
Cassiopeia in her chair,
  And spangle-decked Orion:

While single gems of brilliant light
  Flash out beyond the others—
Aldebaran, Capella bright,
  And the Celestial Brothers.

How young and fair they all appear!
  And Earth, could I behold her,
Now in the Springtime of the year,
  Would doubtless seem no older.

And shall not *we* renew our youth,
  As eagles do in story,
And young and fair as they in sooth
  Soar up to God in glory?

How sweet to be a boy again—
  Not what I was, but would be:
The boy I yearned to be in vain,
  But knew I never could be:

The Boy Ideal, strong and brave,
  Endowed with beauty flawless,
Gay as the gales of March, and save
  To Love's sweet law as lawless.

A boy like many a comrade dear,
  Not fallen in war but risen,
Too full of life to linger here,
  Too free for this our prison.

And will it be in Springtime wild,
  Some starry night and stormy,
I'll wing my way, once more a child,
  To the children gone before me?

Maying

Love flew by at the dawn o' the day,
  Glorious, radiant, glowing,
Leaving a light all over the bay
  And setting the cocks a-crowing.
"Up!" cried he, "'Tis the first of May,
Up and away! Away! Away!"
"Nay, Love," said I, "I fain would sleep.
Why do you wake me but to weep?
  I cannot go a-Maying."

Boys ran by at the dawn o' the day
  Filling the world with laughter:
Eagerly running to bathe in the bay,
  But the fairest of all came after.
"On!" cried Love, "'Tis the first of May,
Up and away! Away! Away!"
"Nay Love, why haste? My mother is dead
And never a friend have I," he said,
  "How can *I* go a-Maying?"

Then up rose I at the dawn o' the day,
  I had done with sorrow and sleeping;
The boys were bathing all over the bay.
  But the fairest of all was weeping.
"Sweet," said I, "'Tis the first of May;
Up and away! Away! Away!
Will you come with me? I am lonely too."
He said with a sob, "I will come with you,"
  So together we went a-Maying.

A Child

His hair is glossy as a horse-chestnut,
   And closely curls about his forehead white:
His features are so delicately cut
   That they would fill a sculptor with delight:
His shadowy eyes are blue and tender, but
   The great black pupils with their stars of light,
Dilating or contracting as they shut
   Or open wide, gleam like the skies at night.
His lightly-bronzed and glowing boyish face
   Is flushed as clouds are at the dawn of day;
And all his form is moulded with such grace
   That seeing it I'm fain to kneel and pray:
   But when I touch, and feel 'tis mortal clay,
I ache to fold it in a close embrace.

The Boy Ideal

I

How often in my solitary rambles
  I see the Boy Ideal on my way,
As Moses saw God's glory in the brambles.

Here as a careless child he rides in play
  Bare-footed on a gate, his laughter riding
Above the whistling winds of March. The day

Is bright though keen: the children round him swinging,
  A ragged troop, are joyous as their chief;
And soaring larks in sympathy are singing:
  What should the Boy Ideal know of grief?

II

One Summer morn I see him as a slender
  But lusty youth, afloat upon his back,
His gently-heaving bosom, white and tender,

Swells out above long strands of glaucous wrack,
  While raven locks, e'en in the water curly,
Spread round his head and form a nimbus black.

The sun is hot, although the hour is early,
  And in its rays he basks with languid mien;
His softly-rounded body, pure and pearly,

Set in a frame of dusky olive-green,
  'Mid viscid jelly-fish and dank sea-flowers,
Laver, dark dulse, and pallid carageen:
  Here he's a merman in his native bowers.

III

In Autumn on a lofty hill that towers
  High o'er long leagues of undulating land,
Below a lurid purple cloud that lowers

With thunder fraught, he heads a joyous band,
  Incarnate as a vagabond, the very
Picture of health, dark-eyed, red-cheeked, sun-tanned.

Intent on loot, marauders blithe and merry,
  Through thorny thickets valiantly they press,
Rifling the brambles of the juicy berry,
  Robbers like Bedouins in the Wilderness.

IV

In Wintertide, as wearily I wander
  Through snowy byways, toward the close of day
I spy an old dark-timbered mansion yonder.

One mullioned window, through the twilight grey
  Gleams like a star: within, on raftered ceiling

And wainscot wall, firelight and shadow play.

Here, through the lattice, with the eerie feeling
   Of one who dreams awake, once more I spy
The Boy Ideal, now an Angel kneeling

Before his bedside Altar. With his eye
   Fixed upon Heav'n, oblivious of beholders,
He's wrapt in prayer: I think I can descry
   Bright gauzy wings around his shapely shoulders!

Montague

My heart went out to Montague;
  Did his respond to mine?
His smile said "Yes;" his eyes did too.
  But still I sought a sign.
I sought a sign the whole day through,
  But 'twas not till the night I knew.
      And how did I divine?
By this—that when we bade adieu
One moment more than others do
  He left his hand in mine.
'Twas as we stood alone, we two,
Beneath the stars with none to view,
For a moment more than others do
  He left his hand in mine.

The Vagabond Boy

Tramp, tramp, tramp,
  I'll not be the first to rest:
I'll tramp it early or late,
  But I like it late the best.
      Give me the moon for a lamp,
        Give me the sky for a dome,
      Give me a lad that I like for a mate,
        And a long white road for a home.

Tramp, tramp, tramp,
  Over the frosty ground:
While night looms big with fate,
  And the villages sleep around.
      Give me the moon for a lamp,
        Give me the sky for a dome,
      Give me a lad that I like for a mate,
        And a long white road for a home.

Tramp, tramp, tramp,
  What is home to me
But a gaol with a wall and a gate?
  I had rather by far be free.
      Give me the moon for a lamp,
        Give me the sky for a dome,
      Give me a lad that I like for a mate,
        And the whole wide world's my home.

Rupert

His mother and I are fellow worshippers,
  His heart is hers as much or more than mine;
But when we play beneath the dusky firs,
  Breast-high in bracken, she can ne'er divine
What 'tis to be a Robin Hood. Not hers
  But mine is he when serpent lightnings shine
And thunder roars, or when the fierce gale stirs
  The rolling surge and drenches us with brine.

An rosy apples on forbidden trees
  Cry "Come and catch me if you dare!" she hears
No witching voice. When o'er the soughing breeze
Blare fife and drum, no beckoning hand appears
To bid her march. O then the boy's my own,
Heart soul and body mine, and mine alone!

A Child of Light

The tide was low: long levels of wet sand
  Mirrored a mackerel sky, green, orange, pink,
With the fiery gleams of opals. On the strand,
  Against the sunlit ocean's shining brink,
I saw a lovely naked boy: his hair
  Was like a glorious casque of burnished gold,
His eyes were stars, his slender form was fair
  With iridescent colours manifold.
Gleaming like mother-of-pearl in parts, it showed
  Semi-transparent; here in the shade, 'twas blue;
Here in the light, like sunset clouds it glowed;
  Here it was amber; here a dusky hue:
Thus decked with rainbow tints, unearthly bright,
  He seemed not mortal, but a child of light.

Warblers

Big bird and little bird warble in the woods:
  Hey tirra lirra! Hey tirra lirra!
Carolling and piping in the merriest of moods:
  O but their sweet songs are sweet!

Stormcock, laverock, willow-wren and thrush,
  Chiff-chaff, blackbird, shufflewing and linnet.
Call to one another out of every tree and bush,
  All about the woodland, over it and in it.

I know a voice, though, prettier than yours:
  Hey tirra lirra! Hey tirra lirra!
Hark to my lad, he is coming out of doors:
  Ah, but his tones are sweet!

Society

I walked with Will through bracken turning brown,
  Pale yellow, orange, dun, and golden-red.
"God made the country and man made the town—
  And woman made Society," he said.

"Last night at dinner, music, poetry, art,
  And worst of all, religion, seemed but shams—
Mere fashionable crazes, fit for smart
  Lip-criticism, jokes, and epigrams."

The morning sun lit up the glistening furze,
  Now veiled by spiders' webs, and wet with dew;
And on the ground lay prickly chestnut-burrs—
  Some split, displayed a glossy nut or two.

Athwart the stillness came a tapping sound,
  And then a bird-like laugh, and presently
A green woodpecker skimmed along the ground,
  And disappeared behind a mighty tree.

There, in a clearing, rose a bushy tail;
  Then down it went to let a small head rise;
And through the grass, a little squirrel frail
  Peeped out at us with brown enquiring eyes.

We roused a hare, that slowly trotted off,
　　Then sat upon his haunches unafraid:
Afar we heard the deer's clear call and cough,
　　And in a glen two fawns together played.

"Last night," I said, "how far away it seems!
　　Society? Nay, that was solitude!
We were alone then, with disturbing dreams;
　　We wake to life and love here in this wood."

My Holiday Home

If I shut my eyes it will all come back
  Just as it was when the June sun shined—
The long low reefs that are dark with wrack,
  The old red sandstone cliffs behind,
The bare-legged children robed in white,
  The butterfly boats in the bay,
The stucco villas, new and bright,
  And the castle old and grey.

If I stop my ears I can catch the breeze
  Soughing around on every side,
And the slumbrous tones of the tranquil seas
  Ebbing away with the falling tide.
But 'tis only in dreams that I *feel* the sand,
  And the wind, and the June sunshine,
And the touch of a hot little sunburnt hand,
  And lips pressed close to mine.

The Fisher Boy

Hark! Hark! List to the fisher boy
  Carolling on like a lark!
Merrily, merrily ripples his melody
  Over the sea in the dark.
Nightingale in the vale
  Hush! Let his song prevail.
          Hark!

Hark! Hark! Who is a richer boy
  Than the gay lad in the barque—
Richer in happiness, innocence, holiness—
  Than the poor child in his sark?
Cherubim, Seraphim
  Listen and learn of him!
          Hark!

Shells

These were Geoff's—no rare examples
  Fit for critical inspection:
Limpets, mussels, whelks are samples.

Here's the best of the collection—
  What he called a "fan," * now faded,
Once as bright as his complexion!

Here's a yellow "token," † graded
  Number One, a perfect treasure
(Cracked in two, and much abraded.)

Well I recollect his pleasure
  When he chanced to find a "Venus;"
And this ear-shell filled the measure!

Is there much to choose between us,
  If it comes to drawing morals?
We're all babes until death wean us!

See that house among the laurels,
  Where the winter sun is shining,
Flashing on the casement quarrels:

Here he lived and died. Repining
  Never can restore the kernel.
That's a shell! A truce to whining;
  After all the soul's eternal.

* Common scallop. *[Bradford's footnote]*
† European cowrie. *[Bradford's footnote]*

The Harvest Moon

O holy moon serenely bright
How fair though art! Yet in thy light
I see a little face as white,
As beautiful, as calm, and quite
      As pure as thine.

Around the world thou runn'st thy race
And show'st thy disk in every place,
But here I kiss a little face
Whose delicate, unearthly grace
      Is mine, all mine!

Expelled

"The young squire's been expelled from school!"
  So ran the rumour. From a child
  The boy had been "rebellious": "wild"
They called him later as a rule.

His widowed mother, pale and thin,
  Was cold and proud as Lucifer:
  I think a sinner was to her
A shade more hateful than his sin!

The boy was prisoned in the park—
  She willed it so I make no doubt.
  With gun or rod he mooned about
From early morning until dark.

"Wild" seemed a curious epithet
  For one so languorous and weak:
  A lad more absolutely meek
And crestfallen I never met.

Yet there was something you might call
  "Wild" in his shifty, furtive eyes—
  The kind of "wildness" you surprise
In those of a trapped animal.

His Summer holidays were passed
  In lounging near a sedgy lake:
  There for long hours he dreamed awake,
And there they found him drowned at last.

In Lynn of old traditions say
  They hanged a criminal of twelve:
  They did not make him hang himself—
They had more mercy in those days!

A Brief Life (A Sonnet Sequence)

THE CASTLE.

The Castle, once a rugged Norman keep,
  Has been transformed into an English home:
Its ancient moat, o'erflown, has formed a deep
  Pellucid pool, where swift and swallow roam;
But where the drawbridge hung, a bridge of stone
  With mossed and lichened piers usurps the place:
The crumbling barbican remains alone,
  An ivied tower whose force has turned to grace.
The level lawns are now with daisies white,
  The meads around with golden cups are gay,
Peace spreads her pinions o'er it day and night,
  And sweet contentment broods there night and day.
The chatelain's a slender orphan boy,
  His mother's pride, my friend, our common joy.

THE VILLAGE.

The village nestles 'neath the parish church,
  A simple fane with one low massy tower:
A purling brook 'mid willow, ash, and birch,
  Meanders down to lend the mill its power;
There, dammed by weirs, it forms a foamy head,
  Where whirling waters, eddying round and round,
Can find no vent, till by the race they're led
  To turn the great black wheel with whirring sound.
Next comes the gabled inn, and last the green,
  Which serves at sunset as a meeting-place
For old and young. There oft my friend is seen;

And ever when he comes on every face
The sunlight of his beauty seems to shine,
　All hearts are glad, but none so glad as mine.

THE GRAMMAR SCHOOL.

The grammar school has grey embattled walls,
　Wide mullioned windows, and escutcheoned gate,
And class-rooms like our smaller college halls
　Where comfort is combined with modest state.
There for four hundred years the happy hum
　Of busy human bees has told of toil
By which the flowers of classic lore become
　The all-devouring scholar's honeyed spoil.
Thither my friend, with rosy farmer's sons,
　The lawyer's lad, the parish doctor's boy,
And other country children, daily runs
　To draw from Rome and Athens' wells with joy.
Yet, loved by all, he lives from all apart;
　They have his presence, I alone his heart.

THE FOREST.

My friend trots by my side in easy pose,
　Head back, hands low, the unneeded whip at rest;
His slender legs, encased in silken hose,
　Against his pony's glossy flanks close pressed:
The evening air with scented limes is sweet,
　The forest glades are still as still can be,

181

The grass is grateful to our horses' feet,
   And all is peace and deep tranquillity.
The wood's our favourite haunt: upspringing elm,
   Aspiring poplar, birch with silver bole,
Broad-branching oak, the monarch of the realm,
   And graceful ash, we love to think, share soul
And heart with us—nay there are moments when
   They seem more near us than our fellow-men.

THE CHURCHYARD.

I knew my darling bore a tainted life,
   And that he suffered for a parent's sin:
To-day I heard that brief would be his strife.
   We passed the churchyard and he drew me in;
He led me to his father's marble tomb—
   A pompous structure 'neath a mighty yew,
Whose shadow bathed it in eternal gloom.
   We gazed in silence; then, as we withdrew,
A little shyly but with quiet pride,
   "They shall not lay me there with him," he said,
"But in yon sunny corner side by side
   Mother and I will rest when we are dead."
And then, more shyly still. "If you agree,
   We'll slumber all together there—we three."

THE LANES.

While he can walk we wander in the lanes:
   At first afar for rarer flowers we roam,
But as his strength with summer slowly wanes,
   We draw our orbits close around his home,
Or sit and listen to the clamourous daws,

Or watch the gauzy dragon-fly, or mark
How briar and thorn bear reddening hips and haws
  And bramble berries grow more plump and dark.
And oft his schoolfellows come one by one,
  Awkward and mute, in country boyish way,
And linger with him till the day is done
  To show the love their tongues could never say.
And now I learn his heart's not less my own
  But rather more since 'tis not mine alone.

THE STARS.

My friend is gone and his sweet mother too,
  They left us with the swallows, and their dust
Lies in the family vault beneath the yew—
  Sinner with sinned against, just with unjust.
My love at last so willed, and I am glad
  He died at peace with all men at the end:
And all he loved, I love: the lawyer's lad,
  A sickly boy, is my especial friend.
And when the night is clear, and there's no moon,
  We roam abroad and gaze upon the stars;
And like to think that we shall journey soon
  To some sweet world nor sin nor folly mars;
And that the stars are lamps that day and night
  Afford our Father's many mansions light.

Autumn Gold

The woods are rich with golden leaves,
  Gold lichen gilds the castle walls,
And on the cottage straw-thatched eaves
  A wealth of golden glory falls,
The mere, aflame with sunset light,
  A molten sea of gold appears;
And golden are my dreams to-night
  For love has crowned my mellow years.

From *Ralph Rawdon: A Story in Verse* (1922)

Book I, Chapter III: Schooldays

ECHO-HAUNTED hollow halls
Resonant with ardent life;
Playing-fields where twilight falls
Lightly over mimic strife:
Reveries of Greece and Rome—
Fancy-love's primeval home:
Turbulence 'neath iron rule,
Form my memories of school.

1

Ill-omened dawns the day when first the child
Goes forth from home's terrestrial paradise;
But in my case the ordeal was mild:
My Eden's borderland was small in size,
Not far, nor famed, nor dread in any wise.
So if my heart-beats quick'nd at the noise
Of five score tongues, while twice a hundred eyes
Encountered mine, when first as boy to boys
I came, the child put off, to share their grief and joys.

2

I felt no fear, and my confiding smile
Disarmed attack. One lad alone, Adair,
Who shared my desk, continued for a while
To scan my face with scrutinizing stare,
But even he wore no unfriendly air.
Anon he kicked me surreptitiously.
I kicked him back. Again he turned a pair

Of big brown eyes upon me quizzingly,
And kicked me harder still. So harder still kicked I.

3

"Can you bear that?" he queried. Lightning quick
He lashed out like a racehorse. White with pain
I bit my lip, and countered with a kick
That made him limp. Adair did not complain,
And all that day we did not spar again.
But after school hours in the playing-field
We fought with fury, each of us in vain
Contending for the palm, until we reeled
Light-headed, sick and faint, but both too proud to yield.

4

Adair was streaming blood; my nether lip
Was like a fountain. As he mopped his face,
My foe observed my wound began to drip
And soil my shirt. At once with knightly grace
He staunched the flow. Then from its turret case
The school bell clamoured. "I must flee!" he cried,
And o'er the darkling field I watched him race.
Then stiff and sore, but cock-a-hoop with pride,
Unconquered and elate, I gaily homeward hied.

5

When next I came to school Adair displayed
A relic rich—a kerchief red with gore!

187

"'Tis stained with blood—your blood and mine," he said.
And ever after bouts of friendly war
He loved to note the bruises that I bore,
And showed me his with pride. But by and by
Another emulation moved us more—
The strife for intellectual empery.
In classics he excelled, in mathematics I.

Book V, Chapter I: Our Life at Milton

HO, ye thirsty! Milk and honey
Purchase without price or money!
Come and buy and eat and live!
Wholesome milk of human kindness,
Honied love of passing fineness—
All we have we freely give.

Wherefore O my friend and neighbour
Wilt thou spend thy gold and labour
For a bliss that soon must cease?
Nothing that this world can proffer
Can compare with what we offer—
Love and liberty and peace!

1

Long years have come and gone since we began
The common life at Milton. First a few
Of Eric's friends agreed to try the plan.
Success brought others. Soon the Abbey grew
Too straight for us: we had to build anew.
A school was founded. Kenneth Ormery
Stayed on as science master. One or two,
Like Guido, left us to be married. Free
To come or go, we live like one great family.

2

"Ama et fac quod vis" the legend runs
Above our portal. Love and liberty
Have ever been the birthright of our sons.
Nor is this love cold Christian charity:
Romantic Fancy, bright, ideal, free,
Though winged and wayward, lightens us with gleams

Of Beauty, Chivalry, and Poetry.
It hovers round our parks and woods and streams:
It glorifies our days and fills our nights with dreams.

3
Our common life, although austere and grave,
Is rather that of scientific men
Than cloistered monks who have but souls to save.
We labour for the world with hand and pen,
Read, think, experiment, and now and then
Go forth on our adventures, errant knights,
To choke Nemœan lions in their dens,
Slay hydras, put Augean slums to rights,
Or wage with Minotaurs fierce single-handed fights.

4
"*Amor' regge senza legge*" is
The motto of our school. It chanced to-day
A new boy came, and when he'd spelt out this,
Our genial Abbot took his breath away
By saying to him (as we always say)
"Who is your guardian-friend? Ah! you have none?"
The new boy stared—he did not know our way.
"Who'll be this boy's Protector?" One by one
Three upper schoolboys rose—Hughs, Willoughby and
    Lunn.

5
"Now then," said Eric, "you can take your choice.
These boys are willing to be friends all three.
Take which you will. Here all the younger boys
Have some Protector, like these lads you see,
Big fellows who look after them. You're free
To change your friend at will and take another,
And he the same. But if you both agree,

And after trial find you suit each other,
You'll be a fag to him, and he'll be like your brother."

6

The little boy stood dubious awhile,
But soon piped out "I'd like to have that one!"
"One more for you!" cried Eric with a smile.
"You must have now at least a dozen, Lunn?"
"I hope to have a score before I've done!"
Laughed Lunn good-naturedly. "Come on, young man,
I'll show you round the school." And thus began
One of those friendships which it is our plan
To foster and direct in every way we can.

Book V, Chapter VI: A Retrospect

"THERE'S a lad full sad;
And after
Trips a boy all joy
And laughter!"
"Welcome both! There's ample room
In my heart for shine and gloom."

"Here's a youth in truth
A hero:
Here's a child as wild
As Nero!"
"Welcome, hero! Welcome lad!
There is room for good and bad."

"Here's a maid afraid
Of many,
Wants a heart apart
From any!"
"Wants the whole? Then she can go—
Let us say—to Jericho!"

1

As I review my life now near its close
I render thanks to Heaven my hands are free
From woman's blood: for I am one of those
Who might have been her deadly enemy
Disguised as lover. Sensuality
Has swayed me little, but the love of grace
Has been my life-long guide, and still I see
This fiery pillar move from place to place,
And its mysterious glow illumes face after face.

2

Could any woman, least of all a wife,
Contented be with love that would not last?
Could she become my friend in after life,
And when her fleeting hour of prime was past,
My confidant in loves that followed fast?
I think of Gœthe's never-ending quest,
His brilliant dawns so quickly overcast,
His Kätchen, Gretchen, Annchen and the rest,
Each for her shining hour his dearest and his best!

3

But if this fancy-love, however pure,
To Woman's cruel, 'tis to Boyhood kind.
Though brief, through briefer youth it will endure,
And when it flies it leaves no sting behind.
And if it lead to friendship of the mind,
This need not pass away when fancy ends:
The friend, unlike the spouse, is not confined
To one alone; but as through life he wends
From many fancy-loves he gathers many friends.

4

Jim, Guido, Ken began a series
Of bright romances. Jim unlocked for me
The Paradise of Beauty. O'er the seas
Fair Guido brought a dream of Italy.
In Ken I hailed heroic poverty,
And found a life-long friend. No love is vain,
Light fancies come and go, for all are free,
But none go empty: and a few remain

Linked soul to soul for aye by Friendship's golden chain.

5

This philanthropic fancy-love of boys
Has been a true phylactery all my days.
Their ever-springing hopes, their simple joys,
The healthful vigour of their sports and plays.
Their truth, the very roughness of their ways,
The frankness of their speech, from flatt'ry free,
Their carelessness, their bold straightforward gaze,
Their courage, and their faith to men like me
Are bracing as a breeze from Heaven's eternal sea!

From *The True Aristocracy* (1923)

E. E. BRADFORD

Chapter XXX: A Peter Pan

Scorning "Society,"
    Bachelor born,
Shall I a friar be
    Shaven and shorn?

Monachal piety
    Could I enjoy?
Had I not better be
    Always a boy?

1

His glimpses of "Society"
Left Edward cold. Those people's way
Seems—first make money. By and by
More money—for the wife. When grey
More money still—for heirs they'll say.
But as I always mean to be
A boy, and live from day to day,
This money-making world I see
Will not mean very much to me.

2

What life then would I lead? I'd go
To foreign lands, and passing through
Adventures parlous, get to know
A host of friends. With them I'd do
Brave deeds, and find out something new
To make this earth more happy. Old
I feared that I must alter too,
And grow like greybeards grave and cold:
That's worse than death a hundredfold!

3

But why should I? The Rector seems
As young as ever. Every night
His sermons are romantic dreams.
He's far more like a doughty knight
Engaged in an exciting fight
Than just a parson prim and pi.
A battle between Wrong and Right
With friends around and God on high
Might keep me youthful till I die.

4

How wonderful the moonlight was!
He rose. The room seemed bright as day,
And in his wardrobe looking-glass
He saw his ghost. He flung away
His robe, and let the moonbeams play
About his form. How wan and weird
The spectre looked! Dark shadows lay
Around it, and he almost feared
'Twould melt, so fragile it appeared.

5

He raised the window-sash. How still
Was all outside! Row after row
Pale phantom houses crowned the hill
With moonlight on their roofs like snow.
Then came the pine wood; but below,
Between the trees, a little track
Of silver ran. He saw it go
Across the hill to one far back—

A thread of white against the black.

6

"That leads—? But roads lead everywhere!
When I am ripe for heaven some night
That narrow path may lead me there.
I'll don my shroud." Arrayed in white
He humbly knelt and said a prayer.
"And now to all the world I'll die.
We feeble mortals cannot bear
An endless life, so Death draws nigh
Each night and in his arms we lie!"

Chapter LI: What Is Man?

My crown and sceptre laid aside,
  I smile at regal vanity:
Henceforward all my modest pride
  Shall be in my humanity.

1

The sun had set when Edward went:
Alone a wan, reflected light
Still lingered in the sky, and lent
Day's glamour to the peace of night.
The twilight town looked strangely white.
It seemed to Edward he had passed
From earth into a world more bright,
More open to romance, more vast,
And far more joyous than the last.

2

A band of fisherboys went by:
He smiled to think in days of yore
They moved his curiosity
As beings strange! All that was o'er.
They were his peers no less or more
Than Dick himself. He climbed the hill
That rose abruptly from the shore
Behind their cove. Though calm and still
The Autumn night was turning chill.

3

But Edward's heart was warm. He lay
Full length upon the burnt-up grass
That clothed the cliff. In dreamy way
He saw, as in a magic glass,

His life—a quest of friendship—pass
Before his eyes. Here first came Clare.
How delicately pure he was!
He seemed the Child Ideal, fair
And undefiled, and free from care.

4

Then Clifford followed—Puberty,
With the impurities that mar
Rank growths of love. Last of the three,
And yet already dearest far,
Came Dick, the Man, who could unbar
Pride's prison and free Edward's soul.
"How small the vain distinctions are
Of rank! Humanity's one whole:
We have one starting point, one goal!"

From *The Tree of Knowledge* (1925)

Canto IX: Friendship

I

Philip and I have been friends from youth,
  And never another like Philip found I.
And what should I want with another, in sooth
  While Philip himself was by?

For Philip is all in all to me—
  Father and mother and child and wife:
His face is the last on earth I'd see,
  And the first in the future life!

II

On holidays Ray loved to go
Long rambles all alone with Ro.
Perhaps some Winter afternoon
They'd climb a lofty hill, and soon,
Head close to head, and arms entwined,
Leave all the workday world behind
And drift away to dreamland. Ray,
Who always had the most to say,
Would make up tales of what they two
When they were grown up men would do.

As Ro's excitement grew and grew,
His twitching arm would hug more tight.
At times to show extreme delight,
An errant hand would seize an ear
And fondle it. This seemed to cheer
The storyteller, as applause

The actor, and without a pause
The tales went on. If they were late
The punishment that was their fate
Seemed part of the adventure. Both
Endured together, nothing loth.

III
SONG: WIND AND WET.

Chorus: Wind and wet, wind and wet,
         Where's the harm in wind and wet?

    Windy all around him,
      Wet the pier below him,
    Thus it was I found him,
      Thus I got to know him.

    Fishing all the day there,
      Fishing half the night, too;
    If I liked to stay there
      Had I not a right to?

    Windy from the first, Sir;
      Wet before the end, Sir;
    When they both were worst, Sir,
      Then I won my friend, Sir!

Canto XVI: Romantic Friendship

I

Boys' ardent friendships some esteem
    Mere whimsicality;
At times to pedagogues they seem
    An abnormality.

Yet, if unchecked, we have to own
    They soon will spread to all:
'Tis strange if Nature left alone
    Becomes unnatural!

II

As Owen joined the house where Ray
Was captain, in the usual way
He had to fag for him. Ere long
He learnt the sweetness of the strong.
Ray took to him at once, but yet
The big boy never seemed to pet
The youngster. Nay, in schoolboy style
He'd scold and bluster: but his smile
Took off the sting; and when alone
He dropped his domineering tone.

While Owen, though reserved and shy
With others, laid his prudence by
With him, and chattered freely. Then
Ray let him see that boys and men
Can be as tender in their way
As any woman. Day by day

Their friendship grew. If Owen now
Had fits of rage, Ray showed him how
The fault was often half his own;
And griefs that, brooded on alone,
Grew thunderclouds, with sunny Ray
Like morning mist would melt away.

III

Sun is welcome in the Spring
    While its heat is rare;
Birds delight ere many sing;
    Early flowers are fair.

How we thrill when in the wood
    Violets we greet!
And after boyhood's Winter rude
    Oh, how first love is sweet!

Canto XVII: Gleams of Sunshine

I

Boys' beauty is as brief alas!
As that of frostwork on the glass,
That's hardly seen before the ray
That shows it makes it melt away.
But though 'tis brief, what beauty can compare
With this—so strangely, delicately fair!

II

Soon Owen, patronized by Ray,
Became in lower schoolboy way
A budding "blood." Good looks and wit
Began to tell. Ray, seeing it,
Gave skilled advice. The grateful boy
Received these hints with fearful joy,
And when his money failed, to get
All Ray suggested, ran in debt.
What then? His birthday now was near:
Ten pounds were promised him this year.

III

We watch thro' glist'ning glass,
  Made clear by April rain,
The sun break thro' a mass
  Of cloud—then fade again.

But if we cry "Alas!"
  Unwisely we complain:
It is the clouds that pass—
  The sun will aye remain.

Canto XLIII: Freedom

I

Freedom of soul's a holiday:
     To cast convention off,
Be natural, seem what we are,
     Lay bare each secret part,
Do what we will, and say our say
     Where none reprove or scoff
This is a bliss no use can mar,
     True healing for the heart!

II

Now what appeared of old at Chaye
A hopeless dream became for Ray
And Owen blest reality.
They lived in perfect friendship, free
From prying eyes and jealousy.
By day they seldom met, 'tis true,
Young Herbert soon found work to do
As clerk at Ware, and Ray with Ro
Pursued his studies. Even so
Each night brought leisure all the more
Delightful for the toil before.

III

Birds in the air have liberty;
Fishes find it in the sea;
Bedouins in Araby;
Outlaws 'neath the greenwood tree.
And I? I'm free where'er I be
If but my friend is there with me!

.

From *The Kingdom Within You and Other Poems* (1927)

A Holiday Land – I

I know a town—but as St. Paul would say
  "If in the body or not I cannot tell"—
Where in what seems perpetual holiday
  Warm-hearted boys and happy children dwell.

Seen from the sea, it spreads out like a fan:
  Low on the left a Norman castle stands,
With donjon keep, drawbridge and barbican,
  While on the right are cliffs and yellow sands.

The centre point's the harbour, mostly full
  Of fishing craft of every build and rig:
No larger vessels touch there as a rule
  Save now and then, perchance, a collier brig.

Above the shipping and the lumbered quay
  Black-timbered roofs with gable ends appear;
And, climbing up the hill behind, you see
  Grey, weather-beaten houses, tier on tier.

A little further back and higher still,
  Surrounded by a wood of dusky pines,
A mighty, square-towered minster crowns the hill
  With blunted spire whereon a vane cock shines.

A Holiday Land – II

Belton is reposeful; Belton looks asleep;
  Belton might be dead to outward seeming:
But Belton is alive, though her quietude is deep,
  And Belton is awake, though she is dreaming.
      Dreaming in the morning of her commerce
        passed away,
      Dreaming in the evening of her riches which
        have fled,
      Dreaming of the dying at the dying of the day,
        And dreaming in the darkness of the dead.

Visitors on holidays who come a while and go
  When Summer sets her glassy sea a-gleaming
Suppose that she is slumbering, but little do they know
  She is dreaming—perpetually dreaming:
      Dreaming of the dying at the dying of the day,
        Dreaming in the darkness of the dead,
      But dreaming after midnight of a darkness rolled
        away,
        And a daybreak where all shadows shall have fled.

A Holiday Land – IV

Every one arriving at the station by the quay,
Emerging from a tunnel through a cliff beside the sea,
  Sees underneath the railway line, and all along the beach
  Lovely little naked fays as far as eye can reach.
Talk about the Greeks' impeccability of form!
Give to me a Belton boy whose flesh and blood are warm!

A curly-headed fisher-lad reclining at his ease,
As handsome as Apollo and as strong as Hercules,
  Is suddenly excited by some cheeky cherubim,
  Who've pelted him with pebbles and exasperated him.
Talk about Discobulus' inimitable grace!
Give to me a Belton boy excited by a chase!

The Early Bathe

Four of us got up at four,
Bent on bathing from the shore.
Nobody could make a fuss,
For nobody was up but us.

Rollicking along the street,
Bertie sang and stamped his feet.
Willie whistled; Paddy played
On a kind of flute he made.

On the green, the grass being soft,
We took our shoes and stockings off;
Long before we reached the sands
All our clothes were in our hands.

Grown-up folk are very well
  When they are agreeable:
All the same it's glorious
  When there's no one up but us!

To a Boy Leaving Home

Ne'er let your eyes with tears be blind,
  Leave all you love without regret.
Run on your course, nor look behind
  Until the sun be set.

If friends depart, ne'er bid them stay,
  Nor chide them if they prove unkind:
On festivals be blithe and gay,
  On fasting days resigned.

And ever bear this truth in mind—
  Eternity contains the past,
And all we lose for God we find
  In God again at last.

From *Strangers and Pilgrims* (1929)

Chapter XLIV: Friendship

True friendship, pure and passionless,
The love that never dies,
Can, by its sweet unworldliness,
Reopen Paradise.

If Alan Dare had felt in fairyland
  When first he followed Fane up Castle Hill,
What did he feel that Sunday night! How grand
  The castle looked! How strangely calm and still
Appeared the sombre pines, now magnified
  To an enchanted forest! How the moon,
Serenely clear and cloudless, glorified
  The sleeping world! His hero, who would soon
Become his mate for life, still seemed to him
  Far off as heaven from earth. He almost feared
Some fiery dragon or some spectre grim
  Would ravish him away. But as he neared
The postern gate his heart beat high with bliss.
  He heard the tinkle of the chapel bell.
The mystic rite would soon make Clinton his,
  Linked heart to heart, as by a magic spell.
They found a doorway, climbed a winding stair,
And reached a little building rude and bare.

Chapter XLV: Partners for Life

How blest are they who, one in will,
  In one high work combine;
And close at first, draw closer still
As they their common task fulfil,
  And share the meed divine!

The jealousies and rivalries
  That worldly friendships mar,
For them have little meaning. Eyes
Fixed on a treasure in the skies,
  Are raised above them far.

And e'en if one to God ascend,
  Before their task be done,
The other toiling to the end
In sweet communion with his friend,
  Will hardly feel alone.

The Norman chapel was a vaulted room,
  Built in the tower, and paved with flags of stone.
One horse-shoe window feebly lit the gloom
  With moonlight saints. Sir Edmund Fane alone
Awaited them. Arrayed in surplice white,
He read aloud the simple ancient rite:

Who shall ascend to the hill of the Lord?
  Or who shall rise up in His Holy place?
He that is true to his plighted word,
  Lowly in heart, and crowned with grace.
He to the heaven of heavens ascends,
Compassed about with faithful friends.

The boys then made their vows, and clasping hands,
   They kissed each other on the lips, and prayed
That God would never loose their loving bands.
   A moment lingering on their knees they stayed,
Then Alan left. It seemed to him that he
Had passed from Time into Eternity.

Chapter LVIII: The Pilgrim Band

> Hand in hand the pilgrim band
> Journey to the Promised Land.

The thought of forming such a pilgrim band
  As might have rescued Joe filled Alan's mind.
The first thing needful was to understand
  Wherein the pilgrim differed from his kind.
The boys consulted with Sir Edmund Fane.
  "He doesn't care for girls," was Pete's suggestion,
But Austin cried: "Misogyny's insane.
  Hate half the human race—" "Hate's not in question.
'Don't care for' isn't hate," objected Clin.
  "For girl, as girl, he feels indifference."
"But that's the way all little boys begin."
  "Yes. And they all are pilgrims in a sense."
Out in the dusk a band of children played.
  Their innocence was not conspicuous.
Their manners and their speech were far from staid:
  They seemed contentious, vain, self-willed like us.
And yet Sir Edmund, as he watched them, saw
  They knew a brighter world than this of ours—
A paradise conformed to Nature's law
  And opulent with wholesome fruits and flowers.
They dwelt in God although they knew it not;
  And at untainted wells of happiness
They slaked their thirst. Their passions might be hot,
  Their ways and words unwise, but none the less
Their hearts were pure. He said: "Sin springs from lust
  According to Saint James. Both Jew and Greek,
Whose ethics mostly turned on what was just,
  Lest this should lead the strong to wrong the weak,

In marriage sought to canalize its stream.
　But Gautama declared the sage's duty
Was to extinguish it; while Plato's dream
　Was to sublime it to the love of Beauty.
Then came the Christ, Who changed our point of view
　From righteousness to love. It seems to me
He taught a form of sublimation, too.
　Was it to something like philanthropy?
Some men, He told us, from their mother's womb
　Were eunuchs born: some were by circumstance:
Some by vocation. This was not a doom
　To be deplored. Rather it would enhance
Their value to the world. This higher life
　Was not for all, however. Those who could
Might well embrace it. For the rest the wife
　And earthly home were suitable and good.
The pilgrim then's a homeless vagabond?
　Nay, he whose only home's on earth is such.
The seeming homeless pilgrim's home's beyond
　The power of all vicissitudes to touch.
Who has no home but that on earth, has none:
　For what he hold's a home, a hostel is.
Who knows he has no home on earth, has one
　Not made with hands, nor circumscribed as this.
For God Himself's his Home, and God is Love,
　And Love and God are here and everywhere.
The pilgrim seeks no other home above,
　But to enlarge his home is all his care."
The boys were silent. Pete caught Clinton's hand.
　But Alan, too completely one with him
To need to show it, seemed to understand
　Sir Edmund best, for in the twilight dim
He played with Austin's hair, as Socrates
Had fondled Phœdon's long ago in Greece.

SONG

"Strangers, whither wander ye?"
  "Whither? None on earth can tell!
This alone is plain to see—
  Here we can no longer dwell!
Elders led, we follow them:
  Cheerily they used to sing
Songs about Jerusalem,
  The city of their King."

"Is there such a place, forsooth?"
  "Nay, we neither know nor care!
If there be, the God of Truth,
  Whom we serve, will bring us there.
Vainly some have sought to guess
  What old prophecies may mean:
Aught beyond the wilderness,
  Eye hath never seen!"

"Stay then! Take your ease with us!"
  "Stay with you in Babylon?
Who are ye who counsel thus?
  Ye, like us, will soon be gone!
See ye not the stream of Time
  Undermines your banks of sand?
Seek with us a surer clime;
  Join our pilgrim band!

He who guides us on our way,
  Like a shepherd leading sheep,
Warning when we go astray,
  Aiding when the path is steep,
Some of those who know Him best,
  Say Himself will be our Home,
Where in spirit we may rest,
  Even while we roam."

E. E. BRADFORD

From *Boyhood* (1930)

E. E. BRADFORD

Boyish Beauty

See that lad, of late a child
Irresponsible and wild,
Now look up with earnest eyes
Tender, passionate and wise!
  Love has lent him for an hour
  Beauty's holy, awful power:
  When he's ripe for toil and pain,
  Love will take it back again.

Boyish beauty comes and goes,
Like a rivulet that flows:
Woman, as a placid pool,
Long is fair if clean and cool.
  Yet the running waters shine
  With a splendour more divine:
  So the fairest woman's grace
  Fades before a boyish face!

Chapter LIV: The Rainbow Round About the Throne

> Though boyhood's glories come and go
>   Like rainbows round a sunlit stream,
> The rivulet will ever flow,
>   The sun will never cease to gleam.

"What shall we say of boyhood on the whole?"
  Frere paused and thought. Below them lay the quay:
The setting sun glowed, like a burning coal,
  Behind a bank of clouds above the sea.
Then, 'mid the breathless stillness of the air,
  A band struck up aboard a pleasure-boat,
Awaking answering echoes everywhere;
  Until the whistle's deep, persistent note
Drowned all beneath the volume of its tone.
  The steamer left the quay. The sun sank down.
A narrow edge of pallid gold alone
  Illumed the cloud, then turned to dingy brown.
"You notice, Hugh," said Frere, "how soon the scene
  Grows bright or dull as gleams or dies the day.
So rapidly does boyhood's mystic sheen
  Illumine life awhile and fade away.
And thus it has for me the fragile grace
  Of all most lovely things—the rose in bloom,
The sunset sky, the love-light on a face.
  These visions of a life beyond the tomb,
These echoes of a half-forgotten song,
  These memories of paradises past
Or foretastes of the Heaven for which we long
  Delight the more because they cannot last.
The boy is ever fresh. From day to day
  His mind expands, his spirit takes new flights,
Some tender charm of childhood fades away,

Some richer gift succeeds. Our fellow knights,
True friends and warriors tried, through life endure.
The page and squire most often come and go.
Their beauty is as fleeting and as pure
As daffodils in Spring, or Winter's snow.
Manhood has power, Age peace: Boyhood alone
The joyous rainbow light around the Throne."

Eyes Lit With the Light of Other Skies

The Joyful Life of Edwin Emmanuel Bradford

1   *'That walk to Berry Pomeroy': childhood*

Edwin Emmanuel Bradford was born into the upper middle class in the southwestern English county of Devon. His mother, Maria Wellman,[1] was from a farming family in Hawkchurch, a village tottering on the border of Devon and Dorset – so much so that it was classed as lying now in one county, now in the other, until being assigned definitively to Devon. In 1844, Maria married Edwin Greenslade Bradford in an Anglican ceremony in her hometown of Hawkchurch. Edwin's family was from the village of Wolborough in Devon.[2] His father James was a watchmaker

---

[1] Maria was born c. 1824, the daughter of George Wellman (1778–1861) and Sarah Stanton (d. 1840s). Her brother James would become a watchmaker and jeweller, professions also prominent in the Bradford family.

[2] Edwin Greenslade was baptised in Wolborough on 27 February 1818, the son of James Bradford (1782–1860) and Betty Bowbeer (1788–1832). Edwin's middle name Greenslade was his maternal grandmother's family name.

all four of whose sons – James, Edwin, Denis and Emmanuel – followed in his trade.

The first four children of Edwin Greenslade Bradford and Maria Wellman were born in Teignmouth, the latter four in Torquay.[3] In 1851 the family were living at 8 Strand, a seaside boulevard in Torquay, with two live-in servants. Edwin was a goldsmith and watchmaker. In 1855 one of his employees, William Easterbrook, was charged with stealing a silver brooch he'd been asked to work on, as well as some tools from the shop. He was found not guilty, but was cautioned not to take his master's property home on loan without permission again.[4] In 1857 the Bradfords' firstborn son, Edwin Reginald, died at the age of nine – the only one of their children to die in childhood. Given the rate of child mortality at the time, this may be a testament to the good standard of living the family enjoyed. One more child was born afterwards: Edwin Emmanuel, the later poet. Born at 9 Strand, Torquay on 21 August 1860,[5] he received the first name originally bestowed on his late brother. His middle name stemmed from his uncle Emmanuel Bowbeer Bradford, who had died at the age of twenty-three.[6]

---

[3] 1851 and 1861 censuses. The children were: Ella Maria (1845–1930), Amelia Hembrew (Minnie) (1846–1918), Edwin Reginald (1848–1857), Louis Henry (1849–1920), George Frank (1851–1929), Ada Bessie (1854–1935), Rosa Kate (1856–1937) and Edwin Emmanuel (1860–1944).

[4] 'Charge of larceny', *Western Times*, Wednesday 21 March 1855, p. 11.

[5] Birth record, General Register Office. The family had moved from 8 to 9 Strand, or owned both premises. The poem 'August. (To a Friend.)' begins: *'I love this month in which we both were born'* – in *The Romance of Truth and Other Poems* (1920). The friend is Samuel Elsworth Cottam (who wrote his initials under the poem in his copy of the book), on whom more below.

[6] Edwin Emmanuel must have been keenly aware of his middle name's significance; he was to write about the Bible text 'Emmanuel, which being interpreted is, God with us' (Matthew 1:23) in *Sermon Sketches for the Sundays of the Christian Year* (1907), pp. 36–40.

Edwin Emmanuel was baptised at St Luke's Church, Warren Hill, Torquay. In 1861, the family was living at 9 Strand, his father listed as a goldsmith and marble mason. Living in with the family were a cook, a nurse and a housemaid. The 1871 census is the final snapshot of the family with the parents alive. Edwin Sr is recorded as a jeweller and silversmith, assisted by his eldest daughters Ella and Amelia. Son George Frank is not at home; the other four children, down to ten-year-old Edwin Emmanuel, are in school. There are two servants. Young Edwin boarded at The Castle College, a preparatory school perched on a rocky eminence in Torquay where learning was imparted to 'the sons of gentlemen only between the ages of seven and fourteen'.[7] The school advertised Torquay's mild climate as 'specially suited for the residence of delicate and Indian Boys'. Castle prepared its pupils for the public schools, the Royal Navy and other examinations; it made good on its reputation in the case of Edwin, who would go up to Oxford.

---

[7] Edwin Emmanuel having gone to Castle is recorded in Foster (1893). Foster refers to Bradford's father as 'Edward Greendale [sic], gent.', and other records qualify both Edwin Sr's brothers and Edwin Jr's brothers as such. Variously defined, the qualification 'gentleman' originally referred to the lowest rank of the landed gentry and, in a broad sense, indicated that one was able to live on one's private means.

E. E. BRADFORD

The Castle College (also called The Castle School), Torquay

Advertisement for The Castle School, Torquay, c. 1890

Bradford's poetry divulges a thing or two about his childhood. Caution must be exercised when sifting a person's artistic output for autobiographical information. While his poems are usually personal in tone, expressing thoughts and experiences in the first person, one generally can't be sure what is based on actual experience and which events and persons were given shape by the imagination. Sometimes, however, indications go strongly one way or the other. Bradford liked citing boys' names in his poems – a key factor in enhancing their immediacy and appeal – and such names seem clearly invented when particularly euphonic and helpful for the rhyme (*'Returning from Church on a fine June night, / With a shy little fellow called Merrivale White'*; *'O Paddy Maloy is a broth of a boy'*). In other cases, events recounted concur with the known biography (e.g., the travelogue poem 'In Quest of Love' mentions a visit to Switzerland, and a resident of Nordelph where Bradford was parish priest recalled that the Reverend visited Switzerland[8]), and it is reasonable to assume their general agreement with his actual life.

With this in mind, there is every possibility that Bradford was writing autobiographically when he recalled in the poem 'Boy Friends'[9] that on first going to boarding school, he thought the term would never end. But he made a friend, Jack, who on a walk with him to Berry Pomeroy – a ruined castle several miles inland from Torquay – told him where each ship seen down in the bay was bound, showed him the castle's dungeons and, at dusk, pointed out the stars. On the way home, the talk was 'of life and love and God'. Bradford remembered the walk with Jack as a key event in his development: *'And now it always seems to me / That walk to Berry Pomeroy / Marks out just when I ceased to be /*

---

[8] The poem opens out the collection *In Quest of Love and Other Poems* (1914); Bradford's visit to Switzerland was mentioned by Nordelph resident Chris Manning to Knott (2005).
[9] *Sonnets Songs & Ballads* (1908), p. 126.

A child, and first became a boy!'[10] An alternative take, of course, is that this castle ruin – a stiff walk indeed from Torquay – was chosen as a happy rhyme for 'boy'. In the aforementioned travel poem 'In Quest of Love', he confides another apparent boyhood recollection: *'My friend, a merry Irish boy, / Made sport of all. In careless play / We passed the livelong summer's day, / And Love seemed but an idle toy. // But once, as on the sands we lay, / We kissed: and thereupon a flame / Of passion pure that knows no shame / Showed love full-grown. March passed to May // Without an April.'* He goes on to call this friend the first and last love of his boyhood.

On 1 September 1873, when Edwin had just turned thirteen, his mother Maria died of liver disease.[11] *'One night,'* he later recalled, *'I raised a mound of pillows high / To represent her form, that I might cry / As 'twere upon her bosom.'*[12] Following this loss, his father's mental and physical health took a downward turn. Edwin Sr began to suffer from a pain in his throat, which he felt was going up into his head. He would often hear a voice that said: "What are you doing here? One half of you is buried in the grave." He made one of his daughters promise that if he went out of his mind, she would not send him to an asylum. His own father, James, was once placed under restraint for insanity and ended his days in a lunatic asylum.[13] On 16 May 1874, shortly before midnight, Edwin Greenslade Bradford snuck out of bed and took a bread knife to his own tormented throat. The next morn-

---

[10] For Bradford, as his poetry makes clear, boyhood had a special quality of purity and divinity; it was not just an age range, but a state to which to aspire all one's life. His experience with Jack was his initiation into this state.

[11] Death record, General Register Office. She died at home, 9 Strand, aged forty-eight.

[12] 'Humour and Pathos', *In Quest of Love and Other Poems* (1914), p. 72.

[13] James Bradford was admitted to Plympton House in Plymouth on 7 September 1860 – his grandson Edwin Emmanuel was two weeks old – and died there a mere ten days later (The National Archives; Commissioners in Lunacy, 1845–1913. Lunacy Patients Admission Registers).

ing, a recently hired domestic servant found him bled out on the landing.[14] Orphaned at the age of thirteen, Edwin Jr – insofar as he wasn't at boarding school – would have been left in the care of his elder siblings and perhaps of his uncles Denis and James, who had been trading on nearby Victoria Parade (jewels fashioned by the Bradfords still come up for sale). At the time of the 1891 census, four of his siblings still lived at the parental address, 9 Strand, where his eldest sister Ella had continued her father's jewellery business.

2 *'Love shone around me': Oxford and the pilgrimage years*

Bradford, freshly turned twenty-one, entered Exeter College at Oxford University in October 1881 to study theology,[15] his two elder brothers having gone to the same college before him. In June of that year, seventeen-year-old Samuel Elsworth Cottam from Manchester had enrolled there; he and Bradford became lifelong friends,[16] and Cottam's 1930 collection *Cameos of Boyhood*

---

[14] 'Suicide of a Torquay Tradesman', *Torquay Times and South Devon Advertiser*, 23 May 1874, p. 5 – a detailed report on the suicide of Edwin Greenslade Bradford and the circumstances leading up to it.

[15] *Oxford University Gazette*, vol. 12, 1882, p. 62.

[16] This characterisation, repeated from source to source, derives from Bradford's printed dedication in *Passing the Love of Women and Other Poems* (1913): 'Dedicated to his lifelong friend, Rev. S. E. Cottam, A.M. Coll.-Exon., Oxon.' The volume opens with the Elizabethan sonnet 'To My Friend, S. E. C.', about the recognition that Cottam's praise is not mere flattery. The poem 'Passing Fancies' declares: *'O happy he / Who 'mid a hundred lovers, / Ere Fancy flee / One faithful friend discovers!'* (p. 21). In the poem 'The Turning-Point', the line *'So now, fair friend, I'll cease to be your lover'*, if not necessarily addressed to Cottam, admits speculation that he and Bradford were lovers as undergraduates (p. 53).

and Other Poems was to earn him his own star in the Uranian pantheon. The English universities at this time had a thriving homosexual subculture fed by the public schools, with close social contact between dons and undergraduates.[17, 18] Philhellenist-inspired homosociality was prevalent particularly at Oxford at the time Bradford was there. What's more, the Oxford Movement, a circle of men who sought to associate the Anglican Church more closely with Roman Catholicism, was devoted to classical culture and was suspected of harbouring homosexual sympathies.[19] Bradford, too, started out an Anglo-Catholic.[20] The study of the classical world made it clear that there had been sophisticated civilisations with an entirely different take on same-sex relations, and their intersection with pedagogy, from contemporary Britain's.

It is plausible to seek in this educational environment the root of Bradford's self-confident embrace not just of boy love's acceptability and compatibility with Christianity, but of its uniquely virtuous nature which to him made the love of women look shoddy by comparison. It should also be kept in mind, however, that when as a boy he and an Irish friend kissed on the sands (as claimed in the poem 'In Quest of Love'), *'a flame / Of passion*

---

[17] Dynes (1990), pp. 187-8.
[18] In the summer term of 1884, some Oxford undergraduates and graduates were expelled for intimate involvement with boys of the college choirs. One of the implicated undergraduates, twenty-one-year-old Robert Shelton Bate, had matriculated at Exeter in the same year as Bradford and Cottam. The incident shows both that Greek ideals were being put into practice and that this did not meet with limitless tolerance. From a contemporary handwritten note in a copy of *Boy-Worship*, a 14-page tract published in Oxford in 1880. On these expulsions, see https://www.greek-love.com/index.php/modern-europe/great-britain/not-schools-1800-99/notes-on-hutchinson-s-boy-worship
[19] Aldrich and Wotherspoon (2001), pp. 325 & 486.
[20] Yelton (2009), p. 202. Anglo-Catholicism emphasises the Catholic heritage of the Anglican Communion.

pure that knows no shame / Showed Love full-grown.' The poem
'Side to Side', which may refer to the same friend, says dark sus-
picion marked them out as guilty of a ruthless crime – *'but us nor
doubt nor scorn dismayed'*.[21] In other words, his acceptance of his
own sexuality may have been an instinct predating his time at
university, where it was affirmed and reinforced. Moreover, ra-
ther than causing him to be morally conflicted, Christianity was
central to Bradford's construction of his sexual identity. He saw
beauty on earth as an expression of the divine; the celebration of
beauty therefore equalled the celebration of God.[22] His belief in
the rightness of his sexual identity and of his aesthetic prefer-
ences came from the same self-assured wellspring as his faith in
God, about whom he says: *'God within and God without / Teaches
me this perfect trust. / How can God within me doubt / God without
is true and just?'*[23]

Bradford graduated with a Third Class honours B.A. in Theology
in 1884[24] and took holy orders that same year, becoming a dea-
con in the parish of High Ongar in Essex.[25] His ordination as
priest followed the next year.[26] He was already publishing poetry
at this time: for example, the poem 'Boadicea', not later collect-

---

[21] *Sonnets Songs & Ballads* (1908), p. 29.
[22] As he explained in a letter to the writer Leonard Henry Green: 'all our
conceptions of Him come through His works. The beauty of Nature *sug-
gests* what He is like [...] and the beauty of His children gives us an idea
of His beauty.' Cited in d'Arch Smith (1970), p. 139. In *Sermon Sketches for
the Sundays of the Christian Year* (1907), Bradford writes: 'All who are
fighting for anything right against anything wrong are on the side of the
God of truth and beauty and order' (pp. 59-60).
[23] 'The Kingdom Within You', *The Kingdom Within You and Other Poems*
(1927), p. 6.
[24] Foster (1893).
[25] 'Ordination by the Bishop of St. Albans', *The Herts Advertiser and St.
Albans Times*, 27 December 1884, p. 5.
[26] 'Ordinations', *Morning Post*, 22 December 1885, p. 2.

ed, appeared in *London Society*.[27] He also played the piano and organ;[28] if this was not an integral part of the skills taught to the clergy, it must have formed part of his good upbringing. At the start of 1887 he was appointed curate of St Saviour's, Walthamstow, a fast-growing parish now in East London.[29] The reference must be to London when in his travel poem 'In Quest of Love' he writes: *'In that old city, ever young [...] I sought the love that David sung. [...] A few I found, yet found I few / Who knew the love that brings no tears.'*[30]

Before the year was out he became assistant chaplain in the Anglican church in Saint Petersburg, Russia, where he stayed until 1889.[31] Anyone who wishes to speculate that Bradford may have left a given parish or location in the wake of a scandal (or to forestall one) is free to do so, but there is no record of any such controversy ever attaching to him. He waxes lyrical about Saint Petersburg and its inhabitants in 'In Quest of Love' – and in these lines there speak a love and admiration for mankind that we find repeatedly in his work:

> *And Love illumed that Northern strand*
> *Where three brief years I made my home.*

---

[27] *London Society: An Illustrated Magazine*, vol. XLVIII, 1885, p. 607.

[28] 'Ongar Cricket Club', *Chelmsford Chronicle*, 21 May 1886, p. 6. At the club's annual concert, Mrs. Cunnah and the Rev. E. E. Bradford played a well-received violin and piano duet (the movement 'Allegro Piacevole' from Beethoven's Sonata in A Major, opus 12).

[29] 'Licences to Curacies', *Manchester Courier*, 13 January 1887, p. 3.

[30] 'In Quest of Love' is a 165-quatrain tour de force in which, within each of its 17 divisions, the inner lines of each quatrain rhyme with the outer lines of the next. It presents the poet as a well-travelled man who enjoyed seeing the world and interacting with it.

[31] Foster (1893). One of the persons to correspond with Bradford later about Bradford's poetry, the Rev. John Frank Buxton (1852–1942), was assistant chaplain in Saint Petersburg from 1881 to 1885 – d'Arch Smith (2017), p. 395.

No brighter shines the golden dome
Of Isaac's vast cathedral grand,[32]

That like a star above the foam
     Of Finland's fretful waters gleams,[33]
     Than shines the Love that haunts the dreams
Of mystic Slavs. Dark as the loam

That forms their virgin soil, and teems
     With riches inexhaustible,
     Their hearts volcanic, deep as hell,
Are treasuries from whence there streams

The crystal fount of Friendship. Fell
     Their wrath may blaze, and passionate
     Against injustice burns their hate,
But all who learn to love them well

Find underneath their fight with fate
     An ardour for humanity,
     A love in essence heavenly,
Selfless, sublime, immaculate.

It is to his stay in Russia that we owe such ballads as 'The Russian Conscript', '"So as by Fire"' (*'Sidney Swann, the motor-driver, when a lad of seventeen, / Went to Russia with his master, Count Dmitri Galitzin'*), 'The Russian Cobbler' and 'Ivàn and Yefim', all from his first collection, and such stories as 'The land of the Tsars: A Holiday Adventure' and 'Bear Hunting In Russia and Out of It'. His stories began to appear in boys' magazines – *The Captain, Chatterbox, The Boy's Own Paper, Young England, Young Men* – by the 1890s, well before his poetry collections came out. Perhaps he contributed stories from abroad to foster a sense of connection with his home country, or he thought that

---

[32] Saint Isaac's Cathedral, Saint Petersburg.
[33] Saint Petersburg lies on the Gulf of Finland.

as a traveller he was well-placed to entertain and edify young readers with tales of travel and adventure. The stories are short, competently written yarns, agreeable and witty if sometimes high on pathos, set in different countries. Gallant friendships and exalted sentiments between boys form a common thread; the theme of a boy befriending and protecting a smaller, weaker boy crops up more than once. Bradford will himself have read his way through a fair share of adventure stories as a boy, writing later: *'Many an expedition strange / I dreamed of as a boy: I know not how / I drifted to this life of contemplation.'*[34]

The Boy's Own Paper.

OUR TRIP TO MYCENÆ.

By the Rev. E. E. Bradford, b.a.

CHAPTER II.

I'T's an awfully pretty line from Patras to Corinth; you go all along by the Gulf, which is so narrow that it looks like a river. Generally the train runs along close to the shore, and you can watch the fellows bathing on the sands, or fishing from funny little huts suspended over the sea on the top of long wooden stilts. Sometimes it sweeps up a little higher on the side of a hill, where you can only

Corinth at about one o'clock. As we were to stop here for more than three hours before going on to Athens, Ronald suggested that instead of having anything at the railway buffet we should go into the town and order luncheon at one of the *xenodocheia* or inns.

New Corinth is close to the sea, about three miles and a half from the old city.

along. Lawrie," said Ronald. "The train for Phychtia starts at quarter-past two. I shall just catch it if I look sharp. You go on and secure me a corner seat, will you, while I take my ticket."

I laughed at the idea of the train being so crowded that such a precaution should be necessary, but, as Ronald seemed rather excited, I did as directed. He was a very long time taking his ticket, and when at last he appeared, the train was just on the point of starting. I was standing at the open door of an empty carriage which I was guarding for him, and was just going to jump down on to the platform as he came up, when to my amazement he gave me a violent push back, and, getting in himself, slammed the door after him. At the same moment the engine gave a sharp whistle, and the train was off!

I was furious when I saw the trick Ronald had played me, but he only burst out laughing, saying, "There's your ticket, old man! You didn't suppose I was going to leave you behind to tell Carey and spoil all the fun, did you? Rather not! Why, the best of the joke is that he won't know what has become of us!"

Bradford's serial 'Our Trip to Mycenæ' appeared in
The Boy's Own Paper *in 1896.*

In 'Bear Hunting In Russia and Out of It', published in the *Chatterbox Christmas-box* annual for 1900, the narrator is invited over to Russia by his uncle, a consul at Saint Petersburg. Because the uncle knows him and the schoolboy Reggie Edwards to be

---

[34] 'Shades of Night', *Lays of Love and Life* (1916), p. 155.

'inseparables', the latter is also invited. Reggie is nicknamed Monkey because he's always up to some monkey trick, and in turn calls his friend an old bear for sometimes acting bearish to him. During a snowball fight out in the country the two get lost in the forest and, with a bear in hot pursuit, flee up a pine tree. I don't propose that this particular adventure might be autobiographical, but where the two heroes travel to the Valdai Hills between Saint Petersburg and Moscow and the narrator proclaims these hills 'a swindle—such gentle slopes that you hardly know when you are at the top or when you are at the bottom', Bradford appears to be drawing on his personal recollections and, in this case, to take his revenge on a disappointing geographical feature. Likewise, it is Bradford the traveller who speaks in 'A Boy Isvoschik', a *Chatterbox* story from 1895, of 'that peculiarly gentle expression one so often sees in young Russians, especially among the peasantry'. In this story an Englishman hails a ride from a desperately poor teenage *isvoschik*, or sledge-driver, in Saint Petersburg.

Another tale of Russian inspiration, 'Boris Orloff', appeared in *The Boy's Own Paper*, a magazine published by the Religious Tract Society to which Bradford contributed various stories. Originally published in 1893, this story is notable because it was posthumously reissued in 1968 as *Boris Orloff: A Christmas Yarn* in a limited edition by antiquarian bookseller and Uranian biographer Timothy d'Arch Smith. It was again reprinted in 2006, together with the story 'The Fete at Peterhof', as *St Petersburg Boys* in a limited edition by antiquarian bookseller Callum James. 'Boris Orloff' is narrated by an English adolescent who embarks on a romantic friendship with Artie, a boy a few years younger. To his and Artie's mutual distress, the narrator is sent to live with his father, first secretary to the British embassy at Saint Petersburg. Here he befriends a strange, golden-haired, wild little Russian (or in fact Ukrainian) boy 'untouched by western civilisation', Boris Orloff, who looks startlingly like his friend back in England. He writes about his new friend to Artie, and the jealousy thus kindled is eventually resolved in a dramatic way.

From his appointment in Saint Petersburg, Bradford moved on to Paris, where in 1890 he joined St George's Anglican Church in rue des Bassins.[35] The Anglican community in Paris had taken this new church building in use just over a year before his arrival; it was French Byzantine in style and looked rather grand, with an interior gallery, rose windows and mosaics.[36] Here Bradford served as assistant curate under the Reverend George Washington, a descendant of the American Founding Father.[37] Recently arrived, Bradford was one of the two clergymen who read the service at the funeral of art collector, benefactor and Francophile Sir Richard Wallace, who had been intimately connected with St George's, in July 1890.[38] Bradford's friend Samuel Elsworth Cottam, first met when both were undergraduates, was also an assistant curate at St George's at the time Bradford was there, although apparently for a much shorter period.[39] It's a logical assumption that Cottam sought employment with St George's because Bradford was there, and the latter may have recommended him. As Anglo-Catholics, the two would have felt at home there, the church having been clearly 'built for liturgy of the anglo-catholic tradition'.[40] This may be one reason, in fact, why Bradford stayed on for the rest of the decade.

---

[35] *The Clergy List, with which is Incorporated the Clerical Guide and Ecclesiastical Directory* (1897), London: Kelly and Co., Limited. Rue des Bassins was renamed rue Auguste Vacquerie in 1895.

[36] Harrison (2005), p. 40.

[37] Ibid., pp. 48-51.

[38] 'Funeral of Sir Richard Wallace', *The Globe*, 24 July 1890, p. 3.

[39] 'For a while there was also a second assistant, the Rev'd Samuel Cottam, whom Bradford knew from their time as undergraduates' – Harrison (2005), p. 51.

[40] Ibid., p. 47.

Cottam became friends with one of the choirboys of St George's, the son of a prominent English hatter in Paris, who was to become his literary executor and to edit his posthumous *Friends of My Fancy and Other Poems* (1960).[41] This felicitous friend, Leonard Ashley Willoughby (1885–1977), became professor of German at the University of London and a Goethe specialist, and donated Cottam's collection of Uranian materials to the British Museum.[42] Willoughby recalled Bradford and Cottam as 'men of taste and learning' who 'were very good to us choirboys'; he also recalled Bradford as a regular contributor to *The Boy's Own Paper*, at the time the favourite reading of Willoughby and the other boys.[43] If Bradford has anything further to show for his time in Paris that has come down to us, it's the fact that back in England he continued to enjoy conversing in French,[44] a language he seems to have acquired through methodical study.[45] Aside from being widely read in English literature from centuries past down to his own time (as is evident from his writings), he read French works such as Hugo's *Les Misérables*[46] and German authors such as Goethe,[47] whether or not in the original.

Curiously, although Bradford lived in Paris much longer than he did in Saint Petersburg, France doesn't seem to have found its way into his writings as much as Russia. He remained at St

---

[41] d'Arch Smith (1970), p. 154.
[42] Kaylor (2010), p. 214.
[43] Willoughby (1957), p. 271.
[44] Hillier (2002), p. 62. A three-stanza poem in French, 'A Jean', is included in *The New Chivalry* (1918), p. 160.
[45] '[H]urried work often has to be done all over again […] if you want to learn a language quickly it is madness to hurry over the elementary grammar rules' – *Sermon Sketches for the Sundays of the Christian Year* (1907), p. 264.
[46] Ibid., p. 243.
[47] 'Love Along the Ages', *In Quest of Love and Other Poems* (1914), p. 60; 'Book V: Later Years, Chapter VI: A Retrospect', *Ralph Rawdon: A Story in Verse* (1922), p. 111.

George's in Paris until 1899, completing a twelve-year stint abroad.[48] His travel poem, 'In Quest of Love', concurs: *'Love shone around me, like the bow / That spanned the Flood, when staff in hand / A pilgrim from my native land, / Twelve years I journeyed to and fro.'* (Bradford liked the pilgrimage motif, and it will return below.) If this poem can be taken on its word, he visited various other destinations in Europe and North Africa – combining, perhaps, the Grand Tour legacy with an exploration of the freedoms afforded by other cultures. He doubtless relied on family

Bradford's friend, fellow curate and fellow Uranian poet Samuel Elsworth Cottam

---

[48] Aldrich and Wotherspoon (2001), p. 67. Cf. Bradford's *Sermon Sketches for the Sundays of the Christian Year* (1907), p. 218: 'During twelve years that I spent on the continent, one of the most common charges which I heard brought against my fellow-countrymen was that they were inclined to be pharisaical.'

money more than on his clerical stipends. In Vienna, he often wandered with *'thoughtful youth or careless boy, / And tasted the pathetic joy / Of fleeting Fancy'*. Finding Vienna a majestic city, he calls Paris dark and chill by contrast. In Switzerland he passed an 'unearthly' summer night at Fribourg, when he shared 'the words of Plato' with two young men and was able to edify them with a sense of the nobility *'Of that high love which lay till then / Deep in the hearts of these young men / Unprized—as pearls lie in the sea.'*

Near the seaside town of Scheveningen, the Netherlands (not the kind of archetypal location, like Italy, or mellifluous placename you'd come up with for a poem if you hadn't been there), he stole upon two boys in the throes of love's madness in the grass by the beach. He *'Surprised their secret (which I wis // Was no great crime) and at a word / Became their friend. For half the day / Beside the dancing waves we lay / As careless as the wild sea-bird.'* In the evening, worn out, the three of them wandered home to The Hague, where Bradford evidently had his lodgings. In Flanders, the occasional youthful fisher held him spellbound for an hour by unfolding the story of his life. Meanwhile, heavy barges piled with bales would crawl down the canal, *'and far the land / Seemed all alive with moving sails.'* Most Flemish boys, says Bradford, are strong, handsome, auburn-headed and tall, with clear blue eyes.

In a park in Brussels, on a holiday, he chanced upon a boy of twelve, frail and nearly blind. Although the boy spoke to him in refined 'French of Paris' (thus outdoing Chaucer's Prioress), he swore like a trooper. Bradford detected beneath his chatter a lonely heart, but *'Set free / The torrent of his love, so long / Pent up, flowed tow'rd me, full and strong, / And when we parted suddenly // As we had met, amid the throng / That filled the pleasure-loving city, / My little comrade, bright and witty, / Haunted, and haunts me, like a song'*. Bradford concludes the anecdote by remarking that he thinks such cases are not rare, and *'Most of the gay deserve our pity!'*[49]

His character sketch of the (typical) Italian boy is complicated, calling his heart *'weak / And womanish; its kindness flecked // By careless cruelty'* and declaring him to be *'of meek / Subservient temper, but withal / Proud'*. Bradford and a party went by barque into the Blue Grotto, a sea cave forming part of the island of Capri. Capri was at the time a prized destination for well-heeled devotees of Greek love. Relaxing naked in the azure sea inside the grotto was a youth who, in the light that filtered in, had 'silvery skin with changeful hue'. The party in the boat gazed on him in awe and, commenting to each other on the marvellous effects of the light, made veiled reference to their admiration for the boy.[50] In Spain, where boys are 'Warm-hearted, brave, and frankly vain', Bradford sat in an inn waiting for his train when a boy divine in beauty joined him at his table, flirted by means of a fan[51] and told him in the available space of twenty minutes *'how he spent / His daily life; what gave him pain, // What joy; where lay his natural bent; / His friends and foes, alive and dead, / And all they did, and all they said. / Believe me, twenty minutes spent // With such a boy sufficed to wed / Our souls for ever! When I rose, /*

---

[49] I.e., most people who seem defiantly carefree have a hidden pain.

[50] This boy bather impressed Bradford not a little. He dedicated a separate sonnet to him, 'The Bather in the Blue Grotto at Capri', in *The New Chivalry and Other Poems* (1918), p. 83. The sonnet in turn has impressed anthologists: it is in Webb (1988), in Kaylor (2010) and indeed in the present volume. Compare also the lines: *'Have you seen boys bathe in the moonlit sea / In the sea-bride town of Italy? // I have seen them once, and I felt almost / As Jacob did, when he met God's host!'* – from 'Canto XLV: Moonlight', *The Tree of Knowledge* (1925), p. 87, and the poem 'Dawn in the Bathing Cove', *The New Chivalry* (1918), p. 42.

[51] Given the need for discretion, 'fan flirtation' was a popular means of conveying coded messages through specific movements of the hand fan. Whether Bradford was capable of deciphering Spanish fan code is anyone's guess.

I shook his hand—but he came close, / Kissed, and incontinently fled.'

The Moors, Arabs and Jews around Tangier, Morocco did not impress Bradford. Using the crass language of ethnic stereotyping of his time, he refers to these 'once proud peoples' as 'knaves void of grace' and 'barbaric hordes'. He laments that love is expressed there in a way he characterises as *'Wild, savage, sensual, stript bare // Of all but primal instinct.'* In Algeria, however, he and a 'pure-blood' Arab lad ascended mount Beni Salàh at sunrise. On high, far from the world and near the skies, they drew together and lay on the springy turf. In a tone that betrayed no self-pity, the boy told him that while still a child he had loved a Frenchman and had himself become 'French in heart and mind'. But the Frenchman had left him, and the boy had resigned himself to his fate in the 'Oriental' way. Bradford's last impression of his companion was formed as they went down the mountain at sunset. The boy carried a gun on his shoulder, his dark eyes keeping watch against surprise, *'For foes grow bold when day is done.'* Did this risky tryst, too, really happen, or should this particular poetic vignette be understood as an Arabian-Nights-like tale, perhaps of a kind doing the rounds among the Uranians? French author and later Nobel laureate André Gide had not yet published his account of his own adventures in Tunisia and Algeria, so his experiences could not have furnished Bradford with a blueprint.[52]

Bradford enjoyed a bright, though brief stay in Greece, where prayer beads fulfilled much the same function as the hand fan in Spain and where he admired the graceful gaiety of Athenian boys gathered in an outdoor theatre. He recalls an instance when a boy dared him to chase him up the steep Acrocorinth, the acro-

---

[52] Gide's autobiography *Si le grain ne meurt (If It Die...)* was not published until the nineteen-twenties; Bradford's *In Quest of Love and Other Poems* appeared in 1914.

polis of ancient Corinth. Indeed, he defied Bradford to kiss him, but never let himself be caught. Turkish boys were rated obsequiously humble by the poet; even so, he confesses he highly prized their love. Near the Outer Bridge spanning the Golden Horn (the primary inlet of the Bosphorus in Istanbul) he often met a barefooted beggar boy, 'clean though ragged'. *'Up the street / On seeing me he wildly raced, / Caressed me, fondled me, embraced— / All for a few piastres. [...] He placed // His cheek on mine, he rubbed my knee, / Tickled my throat, played with my hand— / And all to make me understand / His impecuniosity!'*[53]

Returning to England (*'They love her most, I ween, who furthest roam'*[54]), he concluded that although love existed there, too, it was ignored unless bound by chains of marriage. *'In Britain boys are friendless'*,[55] he declares, lacking kind and true protectors. In these circumstances, he charges in his travel poem, people resorted to defiling love and *'hiring in a fetid den / Its venal substitute.'* Enriched by his experience of many cultures, Bradford looked on his native country *'with eyes / Lit with the light of other skies, / Keen with experience to bore // Through crust of custom'*.

---

[53] Bradford also mentions the Outer Bridge in his 1902 story 'A Dog with a Bad Name'. In a discussion of Ramadan in *Sermon Sketches for the Sundays of the Christian Year* (1907), he notes that this period of fasting 'is very hard on the poor *kaikjis*, or boatmen, at Constantinople, for they are exposed all day to the burning sun, and they work as usual' (p. 92). This aside reinforces the impression that what he writes about Turkey is based on personal observation and experience. Compare also this impressive sentence from the same work: 'Pale, half-starved little creatures in East London courts and alleys; scrofulous, anæmic little beings shut up all the winter in the enervating vitiated air of underground basements of houses in St. Petersburg; ragged, half-starved children who live among the dogs in the slums of Constantinople; naked, ill-fed, uncared for young Arabs in Egypt—yes, all the children I have ever known, have that mysterious hidden fountain of joy always ready to swell up and overflow' (p. 236).

[54] 'Country and Town', *Sonnets Songs & Ballads* (1908), p. 16.

[55] 'The Romance of Youth', *The Romance of Youth and Other Poems* (1920), p. 3.

He went on to do just that, publishing a raft of poetry books that simply had – and have – no truck with the morals prevailing in the society around him.

3   'Only the other side of the house is falling':
     Eton, Upwell, Nordelph

Back in England, Bradford was curate of St. John's, the parish church of Eton, Buckinghamshire (now in Berkshire), from 1899 to 1905.[56] The 1901 census has him living at 128 High Street. He continued to write stories, and the papers listed him as among the reputable authors of storiettes for the boys' magazines.[57] In 1902 his name was described as being ever and anon noticeable in many of the magazines.[58] He resumed his studies, obtaining an M.A. in 1901[59] and a Bachelor of Divinity degree in 1904.[60] On Sundays he would celebrate Holy Communion at 8 a.m., there would be Matins and a sermon at 11 a.m., a children's catechising service at 3 p.m., and Evensong and a sermon at 6:30 p.m.[61] *Who's Who in Gay & Lesbian History* calls his career in the Church of England undistinguished,[62] which must be a reference not to the hard-to-quantify level of satisfaction of his various congregations about his qualities as a preacher and pastor, but

---

[56] Yelton (2009), p. 202.
[57] *Airdrie & Coatbridge Advertiser*, 16 December 1899, p. 2.
[58] *Oxford Chronicle and Reading Gazette*, 14 March 1902, p. 7. The article refers to Bradford as 'superintendent of the Oxford Wesleyan Circuit', confusing him with a William Bradfield who actually held that post.
[59] 'Conferment of Degrees', *Oxford Chronicle and Reading Gazette*, 21 June 1901, p. 11.
[60] *Oxford Chronicle and Reading Gazette*, 24 June 1904, p. 7.
[61] 'Services in Windsor and Eton. Sunday Next, March 20th, 1904', *Windsor and Eton Express*, 19 March 1904, p. 8.
[62] Aldrich and Wotherspoon (2001), pp. 67-8.

rather to his not having risen high in the ecclesiastical ranks, and perhaps to his not having produced an influential theological body of work. True enough, if we put the strong religious element in his poetry to one side, only his first book is theological in nature: *Sermon Sketches for the Sundays of the Christian Year*, published by Skeffington & Son in 1907. The book presents fifty-seven sermon outlines intended as suggestions for young clergymen who are beginning to preach by heart as well as for overworked old salts.

More than anything, the sermon outlines provide a platform for his take on a range of issues suggested by Bible texts. They probably give a fair idea of what he liked to preach about. Some of the notions he sets out are not strictly related to Biblical exegesis, as when at the outset he argues that the old European ideal of chivalry led to the fatuous worship of women. He approvingly cites Saint Paul's remark that it is 'good for a man not to touch a woman'. This is part and parcel of his defence of celibacy for a certain class of men; as he was to express it later in *Strangers and Pilgrims*: '*Promiscuous love, polygamy, one wife, / Have marked the ascent of man. The tendency / Accordingly seems up to single life / For more and more as far as I can see. / All cannot always breed and multiply. / Friendship for some must be the only tie*'.[63] He calls for a New Chivalry, inspired by 'the glorious optimism of Christianity', that does battle on behalf of the weak and the oppressed – whether these be 'fair damsels' or 'starving men, women or children, who perhaps have grown up under conditions which have made physical beauty out of the question.'[64] He further exhorts to joyfulness and cautions against needless

---

[63] 'Chapter XXIII: Free Love', *Strangers and Pilgrims* (1929), p. 41.
[64] *Sermon Sketches for the Sundays of the Christian Year* (1907), p. 15. Bradford's ideal of a New Chivalry – also expressed in his collection *The New Chivalry* (1918) – harkens back to Charles Kains Jackson's essay 'The New Chivalry', published in Jackson's Uranian periodical *The Artist and Journal of Home Culture* in 1894 – d'Arch Smith (1970), pp. 87 & 124.

worry: 'If God be for us who can be against us?'[65] On willpower he says: 'We are so strong in our God-given free-will that all the devils in hell cannot resist us.'[66] Bradford's plucky optimism appears sustained by his ability to create an idiosyncratic, romantic self-concept that infused his life with meaning. In a long poem he describes a fictional clergyman thusly: *The Rector seems / as young as ever. Every night / His sermons are romantic dreams. / He's far more like a doughty knight / Engaged in an exciting fight / Than just a parson prim and pi.*[67]

The sermon outlines are markedly different in tone from Bradford's poems in the sense that the former warn against temptation, evil desires, bad passions and the sins of the flesh, whereas the latter are more typically joyously sensual, whether or not the sensuality is given a spiritual spin. Much depends, of course, on the definition of 'sins of the flesh'; he mentions by name the sin of fornication.[68] Fornication meaning consensual sex between two persons not married to each other, this does not bode well for boy love, since you can't marry a boy.[69] It's more likely that he is thinking about licentiousness between unmarried men and women. However it may be, the impression one gets is that, between these remonstrances against sin (plus the comparatively coy first volume of poetry) and the later poetry, Bradford – perhaps emboldened by his fellow Uranian penmen –

---

[65] *Sermon Sketches for the Sundays of the Christian Year* (1907), p. 29.
[66] Ibid., p. 39.
[67] 'Chapter XXX: A Peter Pan', *The True Aristocracy* (1923), p. 69. 'Pi' (pious) was Eton College slang for sexually puritanical. Bradford may have picked up this term while researching *Stories of Life at Our Great Public Schools* (1908) or while living in Eton.
[68] *Sermon Sketches for the Sundays of the Christian Year* (1907), p. 129.
[69] That said, in *Strangers and Pilgrims* (1929) the friendship between Alan Dare and Clinton Fane, two youths who plan religious careers, is eventually sealed in a chapel ceremony.

'got his courage up'.[70] He may also have taken heart from the changing times and increased liberalism in society, as will be argued below.

Bradford's next curacy was at Christ Church in the village of Upwell, Norfolk, where he stayed from 1905 to 1909.[71] In 1908, twenty-nine fictional vignettes set at different public schools, first featured in *Young England* between 1900 and 1905, were published by Arthur H. Stockwell as *Stories of Life at Our Great Public Schools*.[72] The schools included are: Blundell's, Bradfield, Brighton, Charterhouse, Cheltenham, Christ's Hospital, City of London, Clifton, Dulwich, Eastbourne, Eton, Felsted, Haileybury, Harrow, Highgate, Lancing, The Leys, Marlborough, Merchant Taylors', Mill Hill, Radley, Rugby, Sherborne, Tonbridge, University College, Uppingham, Wellington, Westminster and Winchester. Bradford had visited all twenty-nine, consulting with the schoolboys to verify his details and co-writing each story with a School Captain or Prefect. Dramatic yarns of derring-do and gallantry, the stories bring out local jargon and customs and exude Bradford's 'wonted reverence toward boyhood'.[73] The first one is set at Eton (where he himself, to be clear, was connected not with the college but with the parish church) and tells about fearful new boy Reggie Winton overcoming his tremors to score the winning goal in his first football match, though at the cost of a broken leg.

[70] The phrase used by Eglinton (1964) in contrasting *Sonnets Songs & Ballads* with the later poetry (p. 397).
[71] 'Preferments in Norwich Diocese', *East Anglian Daily Times*, 1 December 1905, p. 4.
[72] Arthur H. Stockwell was to publish Cottam's *Cameos of Boyhood and Other Poems* in 1930.
[73] Watson (1992), pp. 23-4.

My costume consisted of a pair of swimming trunks and about half a gallon of luminous paint!

An illustration from Eagle Annual 5 *(1955). British boys'*
magazines as a forum for boys to focus on the exploits of
other boys and men were popular from the Victorian era
into the 1960s.

Typifying the way Bradford's public-school stories link virtuous activity with an admirable physique,[74] the story set at Radley sees buff older boy Chris sacrificing his own interests to protect others, particularly delicate little Steevie Corda, and in the process becoming an image of Christ – albeit a particularly physical one. Chris is described as follows: *'fair, curly hair, like little ringlets of gold, clustered around his broad white forehead. When his shirt was unbuttoned at the throat, and his sleeves rolled up above the elbows, as they soon were, Steevie could catch a glimpse of his deep broad chest, and see the muscles ripple all over his firm round arms at every movement that he made. But it was his eyes that struck his admirer the most... They had a curious, fearless and loving look, as if they heartily liked everything they rested upon.'*

---

[74] Alderson (1998), pp. 66-7.

Bradford's theme of an adored stronger boy, fearless as a knight, protecting a weaker or younger friend (*'Immaturity / And weakness touch our innate chivalry'*[75]) is entirely in the mould of the school novel genre, which reached its apogee in his lifetime. This genre, much influenced by Thomas Hughes' seminal novel *Tom Brown's School Days* (1857), exemplified the ideals of the movement known as Muscular Christianity. Originating in mid-19th-century England, Muscular Christianity sought to align the faith with physical culture, masculinity, patriotism and self-sacrifice. Its focus on physical health, physical beauty and the male, with opportunities for male bonding in the school setting, was grist to Bradford's mill and will have helped shape the ideals he bears out in his work.

Also in 1908, Bradford's first collection of poetry was published by the prominent firm of Kegan Paul, Trench, Trübner & Company.[76] He undertook to fund *Sonnets Songs & Ballads* himself, paying thirty-eight pounds and five shillings to have five hundred copies printed (his subsequent collections paid their way).[77] Some of the poems had previously appeared in newspapers. His debut collection contains no fewer than seventy-five poems. Given that it shows considerable metrical skill, it is likely that Bradford – who was nearing the age of fifty – had continued to hone his talent since publishing the occasional poem as a young man. In view of the several Russian-themed ballads, he may have written some of the poems as early as his Saint Petersburg days. The volume dwells on a miscellany of dramatic themes, from the boyhood of Saint Dunstan through sailors risking their life at sea,

---

[75] 'Boy-Love', *The New Chivalry and Other Poems* (1918), p. 31.

[76] Kaylor (2010) notes that Kegan Paul also published the Uranians John Addington Symonds, Mark André Raffalovich and Charles Edward Sayle (p. lix).

[77] d'Arch Smith (2001), p. 4, citing as a source the Kegan Paul Archives at University College London. d'Arch Smith (1987) didn't have this information when he wrote that Bradford funded all of his own poetry books himself (p. 36).

to fights with foes that come in the shape now of a mad wolf, now of the bottle. A delightful miniature, 'The Canon and the Chorister', tells of a choirboy who has sung a solo in a crowded church; when afterwards he visits his uncle, a canon, uncle is all ears and they talk of nothing else. At home the boy learns his uncle is about to become a bishop, but uncle had been too modest to mention it and the boy had been full only of himself. Underneath this lesson in modesty shimmers the subtext that the uncle was so delighted to see his nephew and so interested in him that he didn't want to waste time discussing his own career. 'Lines on Seeing a Child Bathing' reflects: *'Some say man's beauty is but bait for love, / As birds in breeding time wear plumage bright: / How can this be, when He who rules above, / Still makes a child like this more fair to sight / Than any woman?'* Although the volume is demure compared to what followed, the homoerotic content – taken as a whole – was plain for those with eyes to see. The critics, at any rate, did not object.

In 1909 followed Bradford's last move, an appointment to a parish of his own. On the nomination of Christ Church rector Charles Francis Townley, he became vicar of Holy Trinity church in the village of Nordelph in Norfolk, very close to his preceding curacy of Upwell.[78] The ecclesiastical parish of Nordelph was created with his appointment. If the village, with a population then as now of a few hundred, lay isolated in the level Fenlands and its church was 'probably the most remote of all Norfolk churches',[79] there is no indication that Bradford was intentionally banished to such remoteness in order to be stowed safely out of sight. Nor is it the case that he pined away in his country parish: when the poet John Betjeman visited him in 1935, Betjeman noted that the Sunday service was fairly well attended, as well as jotting down Bradford's declaration that he was very happy at

---

[78] 'Clerical Appointments', *Norfolk Chronicle*, 13 November 1909, p. 5.
[79] Knott (2005).

Nordelph.[80] The poetry anthology *Men and Boys*, published in 1924, observed: 'He has now been for many years the Vicar of Nordelph. There he enjoys the confidence and respect of all types of people for his saintliness of life and his fearless defense of the love of boys.'[81] According to a grandniece of Bradford's last housekeeper, the Reverend was eccentric but well-loved, and in 2006 elderly people in the area still remembered him with affection.[82]

Nordelph, situated close to the border with Cambridgeshire, lies on the banks of a canal, and the flat surrounding landscape is crisscrossed with drainage channels. In the not terribly distant past, the village had been impoverished and disease-infested; in 1848, a third of the 150 inhabitants contracted cholera before sanitary measures were taken.[83] Betjeman in 1935 described 'a village of 2-storey houses most of them sloping on unsafe foundations'.[84] Holy Trinity church was opened in 1865, built of red brick with a tiny iron spire above the intersection of nave and transepts – 'nothing fancy', in the words of famed architectural historian Nikolaus Pevsner, although he rated the stained-glass east window (depicting the conversion of Saint Paul and the martyrdom of Saint Stephen) excellent. The church was sizeable for the village, with a high and bright interior and light wood furnishings. The Anglican services had competition from the Methodists, whose Victoria Chapel predated Holy Trinity by four years. The vicarage where Bradford lived was also substantial, a tall building with three steeply sloping roofs and several prominent, slender chimneys. In the 1911 census, Bradford was living there with his twenty-seven-year-old cook and housekeeper, Gertrude Mary Bellamy from the nearby hamlet of Lake's End. In

---

[80] Hillier (2002), p. 63.
[81] s.n. [Slocum] (1924), p. 48.
[82] Communication from Jane Crapnell, grandniece of Bradford's housekeeper Sarah Esther Beales, to Knott (2005).
[83] Baker (1851), pp. 552-4.
[84] Hillier (2002), p. 62.

spite of the stately appearance of the vicarage, Betjeman described it as flimsy and its hall as 'dark, grim black line... Terribly poor.' The house was shored up; it was sinking into the ground due to the soil subsidence that plagued the village. Subsidence as a result of the historical drainage of peatlands was an issue across the East Anglian Fenlands. Bradford assured Betjeman it was quite safe where they were sitting: "Only the other side of the house is falling. I'm not bothered."[85] By the time of the 1921 census, Bradford's housekeeper was Anne Maria Watson, aged fifty-three, from Polstead in Suffolk.

Bradford kept busy in his new post. Crowning his formal education, he penned a thesis arguing that Saint Paul contradicts himself on the subject of free will, which earned him a Doctor of

The vicarage at Nordelph, Bradford's home for thirty-four years

---

[85] Ibid.

Bradford outside the school in Nordelph

Divinity degree in 1912.[86] He also set about modifying the environment to suit his tastes. He had the village boys dig a swimming pool next to the vicarage and pile the excavated soil to resemble small mountains to remind him of Switzerland. The diggers, naturally, were rewarded with the right to make use of the pool. Bradford had his goats graze around his little Swiss lake, which he ringed with statues of lions (these can also be seen ringing the vicarage and the school in the images above, defiantly and protectively looking outward).[87]

---

[86] Ibid., p. 63.

[87] Yelton (2009), p. 203. In a version of the story recounted by Betjeman's daughter Candida Lycett Green, Bradford's attempt to dig the swimming pool too close to the vicarage caused the building's foundations to collapse, as a result of which he was forced to move out – Hillier (2002), p. 627.

4   *'My Love Is Like All Lovely Things':*
      Bradford's poetry

Particularly from his second collection onwards, Bradford wrote about his love for boys without an apparent care in the world as to what readers might make of this or what repercussions his outpourings might have.[88] His frankness and extensive output make him a nonpareil troubadour of boy love; not a poet intent on modern experiment, but one steeped in the language of the King James Bible and Shakespeare and reaching back to classical poetic forms, although often expressing himself simply.[89] He is a virtuoso wordsmith, a storyteller poet with – unsurprisingly for an organist – an excellent sense of rhythm and musicality. Occasionally he strays into melodrama, facile lines or jarring rhymes, sometimes his philosophy is belaboured and convoluted, and sometimes he moralises overtly or makes his point too expressly, exclamation marks and all. While one gets the impression that he received little or no editorial help to weed out or improve weak poems, on the whole one cannot help but admire his talent, self-assurance, courage and optimism.

---

[88] The publisher was not scared off by the more explicit content of later volumes: 'the printing bill footed, Kegan Paul did not much care what their authors wrote about' – d'Arch Smith (1987), p. 36. This might have been a different story had a brouhaha erupted over Bradford's poetry, e.g. in the press, but that didn't happen.

[89] Notwithstanding Bradford's preference for classical poetic diction, although he uses informal speech for effect now and again, Norton (1974, 1998) characterises his style as always having 'an undertone of irony that marks him out as a distinctively modern poet.' Webb (1988) refers to the 'cheerful Edwardian charm of a style that can, perhaps, be described as Hinge & Brackett [sic] meet John Betjeman' (p. 11). Eglinton (1964) agrees with a comparison he found somewhere of Bradford to Henry Austin Dobson and W. S. Gilbert (p. 398).

One notion he articulates repeatedly is found more generally among Uranian writers: transient earthly beauty, exemplified by the short-lived splendour of boyhood, is an emblem of divinity and ideal perfection. This is expressed in terms of 'The Child Divine' ('*Methought I saw in visions of the night / The Child Divine, concealed in mortal guise*'),[90] the 'Boy Ideal' ('*For though the boy may pass, the Boy Ideal / Will live for ever*')[91] and a generalised reverence for boyhood ('*Boyhood I worship rather than the boy; / And boyhood but as part of Nature's whole*').[92] For Bradford, childhood is infused with purity and is reflective of the divine; a state that is gradually lost as, growing up, we become mired in sin.[93]

There are recollections and vision-like evocations of seaside towns, likely informed by Bradford's Torquay boyhood (the parental home faced the sea directly). Several such towns feature a castle on a rock, recalling the prep school he attended, Castle College, or perhaps also Berry Pomeroy Castle which he mentions in a poem. The imagined seaside locale at times appears to represent a homecoming, or a prefigurement of the afterlife.[94] The longing for an ideal afterlife suffuses his work, as does a

---

[90] 'The Child Divine', *Sonnets Songs & Ballads* (1908), p. 12.

[91] 'The Romance of Youth', *The Romance of Youth and other Poems* (1920), p. 2. Bradford fashions himself as an iteration of the Boy Ideal: '*How sweet to be a boy again — / Not what I was, but would be: / The boy I yearned to be in vain, / But knew I never could be: // The Boy Ideal, strong and brave, / Endowed with beauty flawless, / Gay as the gales of March, and save / To Love's sweet law as lawless*' – 'A Starry Night', ibid., p. 15.

[92] 'Boyhood', ibid., p. 12.

[93] Children 'have not as yet filled the air around them with clouds of sin to keep off the heavenly sunshine; they have not as yet driven away or greatly hampered the work of that Blessed Spirit Whose fruit is joy' – *Sermon Sketches for the Sundays of the Christian Year* (1907), p. 236.

[94] Anderson and Sutherland (1961) call it 'clearly his version of the Great Good Place' (p. 245), referencing Henry James' 1900 story 'The Great Good Place', in which a harried man finds himself for a time in a dreamlike, restful, restorative environment.

childlike faith that an ideal life will indeed come to pass. People on earth are mere 'strangers and pilgrims' on their way to their true destination: *'Though still I sojourn in this world awhile, / I wear a scallop shell'.*[95] There is bucolic sentiment and the occasional nature poem. There are epigrams and aphorisms, such as on 'Self-respect': *'Conceit's not wrong, though many think it so— / The fault is rating other folks too low.'*[96] There are hymns to God and expressions of religious devotion, which often tend to mysticism. Rather than emphasising Christian dogma, Bradford more than anything expresses a bond with an ineffable God. God is both outside of man and within man. Bradford yearns for the beauty and purity that is God, and which on earth finds supreme expression in the ideal of boyhood. Here and there he turns to classical mythology, such as in the poems 'To Narcissus', 'Jupiter and Ganymede', 'Hercules and Hylas' and 'Apollo and Hyacinthus',[97] but he doesn't go down this path as wholeheartedly as some of the other Uranian writers. His Christian instincts stand like a rood screen between himself and the unreserved embrace of classical culture; he even denounces 'the mistake of the Renaissance in going back to paganism in its search for joy'.[98] He generally prefers to present boy love through an English, Christian prism, often centred on his own time and relating to his own life (whether or not imagined), at other times taking inspiration from English history. Christianity, patriotism and perhaps as simple a factor as a preference for blond boys (the *non angli sed angeli* whom he actually saw around him) inform such lines as *'Talk about the Greeks' impeccability of form! / Give to me a Belton boy whose flesh and blood are warm!'*[99] and *'Is Boy-Love Greek? Far off across the seas / The warm desire of Southern men may be: / But passion freshened by a Northern breeze / Gains in male vigour*

---

[95] 'Stranger and Pilgrim', *The Romance of Youth and Other Poems* (1920), p. 86.
[96] *Lays of Love and Life* (1916), p. 162.
[97] All in *Passing the Love of Women and Other Poems* (1913).
[98] *Sermon Sketches for the Sundays of the Christian Year* (1907), p. 176.
[99] 'A Holiday Land', *The Kingdom Within You and Other Poems* (1927), p. 18.

and in purity. / Our yearning tenderness for boys like these / Has more in it of Christ than Socrates[100] (the latter poem likens the chivalrous protection of immature, weak boys to Christ's sympathy for the disadvantaged). The explicit linking of boy love and Christianity reminds one of the French artist Pierre Joubert (1910–2002), whose drawings depict the gallant, patriotic devotion of happy bands of Boy Scouts to duty, the Catholic faith and each other.

A mosaic in Westminster Cathedral, London, referencing Pope Gregory's reputed exclamation on seeing English slave boys in Rome: 'non angli sed angeli' – 'not Angles, but angels'. Bradford's poems concur, being concerned mostly with the English boys around him.

---

[100] 'Boy-Love', *The New Chivalry and Other Poems* (1918), p. 31.

Notwithstanding Bradford's Christian allegiance, he does ac-knowledge ancient Greece as having provided a paradigm for a nurturing form of man-boy love. He criticises Rome for having debased the Greek heritage: *'I recall / No love like David's for the son of Saul; / But low intrigues with slaves and pampered pages, / And frolicking with freedom—what a fall / From that pure passion sanctioned by her sages / And handed down by Greece to all suc-ceeding ages!'*[101] The poem 'The Call', replete with metaphors de-rived from Greek mythology, identifies Eros as *'The son of Urania born of the sea, / The lover of lads and liberty'* and contrasts him with Aphrodite Pandemos.[102] This references the idea, originating in Plato and harnessed in the 19th century by homosexual authors and activists, that Aphrodite Urania is an epithet, or aspect, of the goddess Aphrodite representing celestial love of body and soul, whereas her epithet Aphrodite Pandemos represents lower, physical lust. (On the basis of this imagery, those English authors and activists who took inspiration from classical Greek pederasty referred to their love as 'Uranian'.) The further contrast in 'The Call' between the boy's natural beauty and woman's reliance on 'powder and paint' has been seen as harking back to conventions in ancient Greek sculpture: 'the archaic, smiling *kouros*, always nude, one foot slightly advanced before the other, and the parallel *kore*, always represented in a heavily pleated floor-length tunic.'[103]

There are ballads, often moralising, which are like rhyming min-iature adventure stories, calling to mind his prose yarns for the boys' magazines. The ballad about Iván saving his friend Boris from a raving mad wolf with one blow of a heavy stone ends on the lesson: *'But turn, with faith for freedom fight, fling be it but one stone: / Thus David put his foe to flight, thus God will rout our own!'*[104] The importance of friendship is an enduring Bradfordian

---

[101] 'The Romance of Youth', *The Romance of Youth and Other Poems* (1920), p. 3.
[102] *The New Chivalry* (1918), p. 5.
[103] Stevenson (2003), p. 207.
[104] 'The Mad Wolf', *Sonnets Songs & Ballads* (1908), p. 62.

theme. The breeze of time-tested friendship is compared favourably with the storm of brief passion, and can even trump the enticements of boy love: *'boy, as boy, is not so inly dear / As man, my fellow-worshipper and peer.'*[105] His hymns to mature friendship (non-sexual, of course) show Bradford to have been far from an isolated *Einzelgänger* – even if his long incumbency in the rural parish of Nordelph conjures up images of isolation – and indicate just how highly he rated the support of intellectual compeers who understood what moved him. He took his friendships seriously and preferred them to be tested by friction rather than remain superficial: 'I feel far more confidence in a true friend after a sharp dispute—you then know the worst as well as the best of him.'[106] Various poems express his view that true friendship is revealed and does not end even if two friends have a major falling-out. This view is bolstered by his faith in God's plan and his trust that failings in the earthly life will be righted in the afterlife.[107]

Whereas Bradford pays tribute to male friendship, women's sexual allure (to other men) rankles with him, and in this he is not alone among the Uranians.[108] He argues that a certain class of

---

[105] 'Boyhood', *The Romance of Youth and Other Poems* (1920), p. 12.

[106] *Sermon Sketches for the Sundays of the Christian Year* (1907), p. 146.

[107] On a friend who now hates him, the speaker in the poem 'A Fallen Friend' says: *'I still am his, / He mine, unceasingly. / Whate'er we say / To-day / Love lives for aye. / We both feel this, / And shall increasingly. [...] When this life's o'er, / Once more / Friends as before / United still / We'll meet − no doubt of it'* – *Lays of Love and Life* (1916), pp. 107-8. *'"True friendship neither can begin nor end. / It is eternal," Fane said thoughtfully. / "A friend's revealed, not made["]'* (spoken by Clinton Fane to his friend Alan Dare) – *Strangers and Pilgrims* (1929), p. 66.

[108] Taylor (1976) identifies 'misogyny and the erotic superiority of pederasty' as one of the dominant motives in the Uranians' work, a trend he explains as a strategy to combat guilt and to push back against society's dictates: 'The Uranians, if they were satisfactorily to formulate in poetic form motivations for guilt-free pederasty, needed to topple from its pedestal the ideal conception of Womanhood which the Victorians erected

woman is bound to entice to base lust men who would otherwise remain devoted to high love and healthy masculinity.[109] He calls for abolishing the procreative imperative, saying 'single life is full as virtuous' as founding a family.[110] The impression one gets is that in his eyes, initiation into the cult of the woman robs young men of their boyhood – that mythic condition in which mankind has the most intense communion with the divine – and thus of their unsullied nature. Bradford's remaining unsullied in that way safeguards his own continued ability as an adult to commune with boyhood,[111] and he exhorts other men to recover this happy ability. Eternal youth is won by forswearing marriage: *'unmarried men / Are always boys! It's only when / We settle down, we age'.*[112] The poem 'The Call' presents the worship of boyhood not as a corollary of a sexual orientation into which one either is or is not born, but as a choice open to all: *'[Eros] is calling aloud to the men— / "Turn away from the wench, with her powder and paint, / And follow the Boy, who is fair as a saint[")]'.*[113] Womankind is not entirely erased in this ideology. The long,

---

as the symbol of acceptable love' (pp. 97-114). We'll extrapolate what Taylor says to the post-Victorian period in which Bradford's poetry books were published.

[109] *'I found a world less scarred by vice / Than by vulgarity. Low plains / Where oft the Scarlet Woman reigns / Veiled as a nun. With judgment nice // She plays with moral problems – strains / Out gnats and swallows camels. Sex / Is all in all to her [...] few are of this type; but small / In number, they can still perplex // The judgment of their sisters; call / Good evil, evil good; and smirch / The fame of manly love'* – 'In Quest of Love', *In Quest of Love and Other Poems* (1914), pp. 11-2.

[110] 'The New Chivalry', *The New Chivalry and Other Poems* (1918), p. 26.

[111] 'Thank heaven I am still a boy in heart' – 'The Earthly Paradise', *In Quest of Love and Other Poems* (1914), p. 44. The association with Peter Pan is inevitable, and Bradford himself recognised the link: *'Scorning "Society," / Bachelor born, / Shall I a friar be / Shaven and shorn? // Monachal piety / Could I enjoy? / Had I not better be / Always a boy?'* – 'Chapter XXX: A Peter Pan', *The True Aristocracy* (1923), p. 68.

[112] 'Chapter XXXII: Eternal Youth', *The True Aristocracy* (1923), p. 75.

[113] *The New Chivalry* (1918), p. 5.

programmatic poem 'The Romance of Youth' suggests that a man who in boyhood has received support and love from a 'help-meet', a companion and helper, is better prepared for a proper relationship with a woman: *'for the boy / So crowned in youth, and early robed in white, / Will look at woman with a purer eye, / And seek from her, in turn, the Love that cannot die.'*[114]

In *Ralph Rawdon: A Story in Verse* (1922) Bradford continues to draw implicitly on the universal historical template of pederasty, where sexual attraction between boys and older boys or men is marshalled in the service of pedagogical and enculturating relationships, which are not just mutually beneficial but integral to the functioning of society, and of which there can be several in the course of a lifetime.[115] He contrasts such relationships with fancies conceived between men and women, which risk leading to lifelong, monogamous marriage that can sour when the passion cools: *'I think of Gœthe's never-ending quest, / His brilliant dawns so quickly overcast, / His Kätchen, Gretchen, Annchen and the rest, / Each for her shining hour his dearest and his best! // But if this fancy-love, however pure, / To Woman's cruel, 'tis to Boyhood kind. / Though brief, through briefer youth it will endure, / And when it flies it leaves no sting behind. / And if it lead to friendship of the mind, / This need not pass away when fancy ends: / The friend, unlike the spouse, is not confined / To one alone; but as through life he wends / From many fancy-loves he gathers many friends.'*[116] Elsewhere, Bradford similarly distinguishes the freedom of male-male friendship from the confining male-female marital bond: *'There's no excuse for jealousy / In manly intercourse; / New friendship's not adultery / Nor matter for divorce.'*[117]

---

[114] 'The Romance of Youth', *The Romance of Youth and Other Poems* (1920), p. 7.
[115] For an examination and overview of the phenomenon from an evolutionary perspective, see Rind and Yuill (2012) and Rind (2016).
[116] 'Book V: Later Years, Chapter VI: A Retrospect', *Ralph Rawdon: A Story in Verse* (1922), p. 111.
[117] 'Chapter XXV: Friendship is Free', *The True Aristocracy* (1923), p. 56.

Notwithstanding such philosophical arguments, the amount of space Bradford consistently devotes in his poetry to putting down girls, women and heterosexual attraction is truly arresting. It is possible that a female rival robbed him of an intimate friendship at one point or other, or that he was disappointed more than once by a boy falling for the opposite sex. But his beef with female sexuality goes deeper than any particular incident. At the risk of treading the quicksand of psychoanalysis, it could be posited that he resolves the conflict between his own sexuality and the predominant religious and social mores by creating in women a scapegoat that takes on whatever is sinful about desire. In fact, it is in religion that he finds justification for his antipathy: *'The fruit by woman given—this alone, / It seems to me, can close the heavenly gate. / The lore that learns is still to me unknown, / I had no thirst for it to satiate. / So in these pleasant glades I linger late / With holy children, and with boys like me / Not free from sin yet from that one sin free.'*[118] He accepts women's struggle for equal rights – then in its first wave – on qualified terms, saying that while women previously appeared more pure and gentle than men, their quest to contend on 'equal terms for equal prize' has diminished their charms and virtues.[119]

The tenor of his verses, argued one contemporary commentator, was not just to denounce the love of women but to do so 'from a perfectly honest belief in their inferiority.'[120] She called for some feminist poet to provide the needed counterblast. The question is whether Bradford's poetry was read widely enough to produce the hoped-for riposte; in addition, the age still allowed for attitudes such as his. Bradford himself was in time moved to write a poem titled 'No Misogynist', which attempts to make his case by clarifying that his deprecation is directed not at women but at a certain type of man – *'the complacent sensualist, / Woman's slave*

---

[118] 'The Earthly Paradise', *In Quest of Love and Other Poems* (1914), p. 44.
[119] 'The New Woman', ibid., p. 42.
[120] Vivian Carter, 'Thoughts on Things Read', *The Bystander*, 2 April 1913, p. 42.

and tool'.[121] In his verse novel *Ralph Rawdon*, the eponymous pro-
tagonist also defends himself from a charge of misogyny.[122] At his
most conciliatory, Bradford concedes that taking a wife is the de-
creed destiny of most men, but maintains that abstaining from
doing so is the purer course of action: *'Sin springs from lust /
According to Saint James. Both Jew and Greek, / Whose ethics
mostly turned on what was just, / Lest this should lead the strong
to wrong the weak, / In marriage sought to canalize its stream. /
But Gautama declared the sage's duty / Was to extinguish it; while
Plato's dream / Was to sublime it to the love of Beauty. / Then
came the Christ, Who changed our point of view / From righteous-
ness to love. [...] This higher life / Was not for all, however. Those
who could / Might well embrace it. For the rest the wife / And
earthly home were suitable and good.'*[123] For all his propensity to
disparage the love of women and his distaste for women's lib, in
his final earthly flourish Bradford left all his possessions to his
female housekeeper. A further irony is that the fourth edition of
the *Oxford Dictionary of Quotations* (1992) included a quotation
from his work which, taken alone, is favourable enough to
women: *'I walked with Will through bracken turning brown, / Pale
yellow, orange, dun, and golden-red. / "God made the country and
man made the town — / And woman made Society," he said.'*[124] It's
the first stanza of 'Society', a poem which ends on the narrator's
observation that the previous night at dinner, in the midst of so-
ciety, he and Will experienced solitude, but now, out on a walk
in the woods, they wake to life and love.

---

[121] *Lays of Love and Life* (1916), p. 62.
[122] *'"You're wrong," said I, "I'm no misogynist. / I'm rather fond of women in
my way."]'* – 'Book III: College Days, Chapter III: A College Symposium',
Ralph Rawdon: A Story in Verse (1922), p. 57.
[123] 'Chapter LVIII: The Pilgrim Band', *Strangers and Pilgrims* (1929),
pp. 112-3.
[124] *The Romance of Youth and Other Poems* (1920), p. 45.

It is in the genre of the love lyric that Bradford delivers several of his best poems. 'When I Went A-Walking', which comes across as something a Provençal troubadour might have written, begins: *'When I went a-walking / In the morning fair, / I met three boys a-running, / And one had golden hair: / Curly locks were they, / Like little rings of light. / I thought of him all day, / And I dreamed of him all night.'*[125] This poem was chosen as the favourite among boy-love verses of various centuries read at a meeting of the Mattachine Society (the American homosexual rights organisation) at the start of the sixties, and was repeatedly called for at later poetry readings.[126] Bradford's general good cheer stands out against the note of plaintiveness and melancholy often encountered in Uranian poetry.[127] In his purely lyrical moods, he expresses a sparkling joy: *'What is my love like? Why, all lovely things! / I see them all in him. When he is gay / He's—let me think—he's like a lark that sings / Soaring aloft to heaven'*,[128] or: *'His mother made his body, Heaven his soul: / And I? I did but teach his heart to beat! / And now his heart hath given me the whole, / And he is mine—all mine from head to feet: / All mine! And O my love, he is so sweet!'*[129] On the rivalry between a boy's mother and his lover/playmate, compare the sonnet 'Rupert', which starts: *'His mother and I are fellow worshippers, / His heart*

---

[125] *Lays of Love and Life* (1916), p. 83.

[126] Eglinton (1964), p. 398.

[127] Bradford saw Biblical warrant for a cheery disposition, commenting on Matthew 6:25 ('Take no thought for your life'): 'the real meaning of our Lord's warning is that we must not be anxious [...] Remember that the Gospels are in no sense a biography of our Blessed Lord. Nearly all His life, including what we should naturally suppose would be all the happiest part of it—His Childhood, Boyhood, Youth, and all His early Manhood, till He entered upon public life, are hardly mentioned. But by far the most important point is that where Christ is the Man of Sorrows He is not our example.' *Sermon Sketches for the Sundays of the Christian Year* (1907), p. 242.

[128] 'My Love Is Like All Lovely Things', *Lays of Love and Life* (1916), p. 110.

[129] 'My Sweetheart', ibid., p. 112.

is her's [sic] as much or more than mine; / But when we play beneath the dusky firs, / Breast-high in bracken, she can ne'er divine / What 'tis to be a Robin Hood'.[130] The staple of the mother-as-rival also features in Bradford's story 'How We Rescued a Slave at Tanjier', published in *The Boy's Own Paper* in 1896, in which a boy arranges for a captain to invite him on a trip in his launch: 'Mother didn't much like the idea; she said she was afraid to trust me to Captain Grey, because he was so "eccentric." She didn't say that when he was here, of course, but afterwards, when she talked it over with father.'

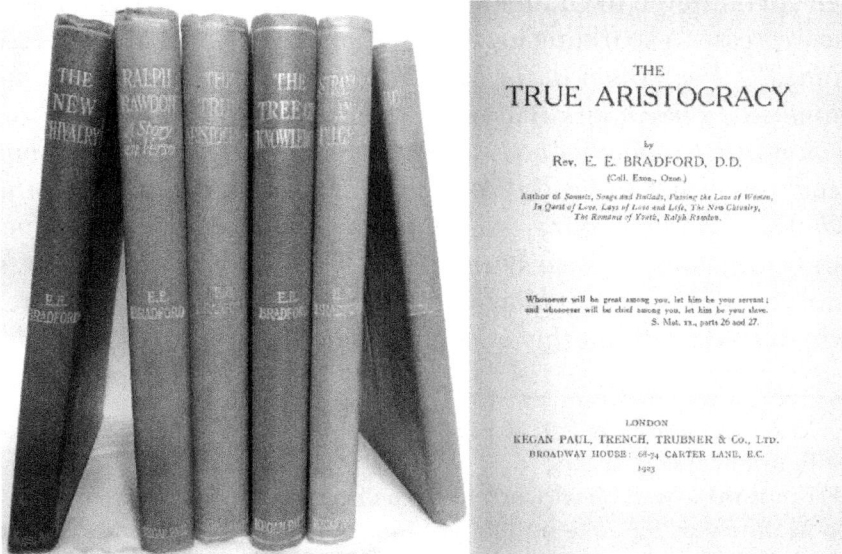

Some of Bradford's poetry books, published by Kegan Paul

---

[130] *The Romance of Youth and Other Poems* (1920), p. 33.

A speciality of Bradford's is to mention the boy he is speaking of by name, which, along with his preference for 'poetry of action',[131] turns many of his poems into enthralling very short stories, a sort of rhymed flash fiction. What Betjeman does with brand names and placenames, Bradford does with boys' names. The speaker in the poems is usually the admirer, friend or lover of a boy, but it's not always clear that he's (much) older than the beloved; Bradford's poetic persona can seem to be an ageless boy himself. 'First Love', which uses a minimum of words to achieve maximum effect, is the touching plaint of a boy who finds the upheaval of being in love for the first time unwelcome: *'Love now? Ah! no. / Love now to me might mean / Man's cares too soon.'*[132]

Over time, the visionary and utopian aspect of Bradford's poetry became more emphatic, and he adopted a different format.[133] All but one of his final six books are short novels in verse, mostly in iambic pentameter, divided into titled chapters or cantos often with an introductory epigram, and featuring novelistic plot development.[134] The form struck Eglinton as being 'apparently original with him',[135] but the genre of the verse novel well predates

---

[131] 'He doesn't merely reflect or gaze upon something, but describes something as it happens and participates in a dramatic situation' – Norton (1974, 1998).

[132] *In Quest of Love and Other Poems* (1914), p. 51.

[133] Kaylor (2010) asserts that 'it would be less than honest to suggest that Edwin Emmanuel Bradford's *Boyhood* (1930) reveals any improvement, stylistically or conceptually, over *Sonnets, Songs & Ballads* (1908), despite the fact that ten volumes of his verse had been published in the interim' (p. xxi). Whether Bradford improved as a poet is open to debate, but Kaylor's statement should not be taken to mean that the content, much less the format, of his poetry remained the same from the first book to the last.

[134] 'To find a book of poetry as readable as any novel is an astonishing experience', wrote the *Dundee Courier* of Bradford's 1930 work *Boyhood* ('Poet of Youth', 4 April 1931, p. 8).

[135] Eglinton (1964), p. 398.

Bradford.[136] Repeatedly, the story lines involve jealousy between two boys vying for friendship with an older boy. In *Ralph Rawdon: A Story in Verse*, a group of friends end up founding a community – comprising an abbey and a school – of men who prefer not to marry: *"'Ama et fac quod vis" the legend runs / Above our portal. Love and liberty / Have ever been the birthright of our sons. / Nor is this love cold Christian charity: / Romantic Fancy, bright, ideal, free, / Though winged and wayward, lightens us with gleams / Of Beauty, Chivalry, and Poetry. / It hovers round our parks and woods and streams: / It glorifies our days and fills our night with dreams.'*[137] Each new boy entering the school chooses a 'Protector' from among the upper schoolboys. *The True Aristocracy* (1923) treats of Edward Neville, scion of a noble family in the fictional seaside town of Belton, a locale that also features in *The Kingdom Within You and Other Poems* (1927). Edward has passionate friendships in childhood, adolescence and early adulthood with boys of varying social stations, and ends up concluding that distinctions of rank are vain and all men are his peers.

Strangers and Pilgrims (1929) recounts the friendship between two boys, Alan Dare and Clinton Fane, who live in another fictional seaside town, Castle Fane. Alan is awakened gradually to Clinton's philosophy that some boys are meant not for marriage with women, but instead for lifelong spiritual friendship with each other. Their friendship is eventually consecrated as a marriage of sorts in a chapel ceremony. The story argues that most people have 'no home but that on earth', but some 'pilgrims', called to a higher life, have their Home in God Himself. These

---

[136] Reade (2017) compares Bradford's verse novels to the narrative poetry of George Crabbe (1754–1832) (p. 53), as did *The Times Literary Supplement* in its review of *Ralph Rawdon: A Story in Verse* (1922) (cited in *The True Aristocracy* (1923), p. 123).
[137] 'Book V: Later Years, Chapter I: Our Life at Milton', *Ralph Rawdon: A Story in Verse* (1922), p. 95.

pilgrims are not encumbered by lustful passions that in others need canalising in conventional heterosexual unions; they can choose instead to solemnise perpetual friendship with each other. As far as can be told, Bradford envisions such pilgrims as being found exclusively among the male sex. The visionary flair of his call for an Edenic chivalry of knights and squires who spurn traditional marriage is expressed in lines such as *'Go, little book, and cry: / Though few at first may heed thee, / Ten thousand by and by / Will gather round and read thee.'*[138] (It is ironic to think how many traditional marriages the Reverend Bradford must have consecrated.) We thus see his poetry running the gamut from playful love lyrics to wildly romantic dreams of social revolution.[139]

Bradford can be different, and sometimes apparently contradictory, from poem to poem. One can select lines that portray him as appreciative of things carnal, lines that advocate idealised love and high-minded chivalry, or, indeed, lines that reject 'lust' and sanction only chaste, spiritual love. He is ambiguous about how he defines fleshly sins and improper lust. Verse such as 'Free Love', which ends on the triumphant cry *'I've kissed young boys in dozens!'*,[140] come across as the creed of a contrarian, even provocative hippie to whom the fallout of the Oscar Wilde trials (not yet twenty years in the past) was ancient history.[141] Then again, there are such declarations as: *'This beauty of the boy, / By God and Nature's plan, / Is not for carnal joy, / But to inspire in man //*

---

[138] 'To My Book', *Lays of Love and Life* (1916), p. 5.

[139] Waters (1995) discusses Bradford's appeal to the rhetoric of patriotic fervour and male energy (in the context of the Great War) to promote his reimagining of the ancient 'paiderastic paradigm' (pp. 67-9). Note, by the way, that it was in the midst of the Great War that he published his collection titled *Lays of Love and Life* (1916).

[140] *In Quest of Love and Other Poems* (1914), p. 43.

[141] Kaylor (2010) notes that 'to examine Uranian publishing history is to discover that *Wilde's trials had little or no negative impact on the movement's publishing history, and perhaps even helped it to flourish*' (p. lviii).

Bright dreams of purity'.[142] And where the poet avers *'I never knew the carnal sting / That prompts to propagate the race'*,[143] is he saying heterosexual sex is not for him, or sex as such is not for him?

While all this ambivalence might suggest that Bradford was grappling with opposing instincts, there is no pained expression of inner conflict, of being torn between his sexuality on the one hand and his conscience, his religion or society's strictures on the other. Whatever case he is making, he sounds self-assured; his is more the voice of a guide and a guru than that of a doubt-racked seeker. Sometimes it seems a middle ground can be found regarding his take on the physical expression of love and desire. He says explicitly, and often enough, that to smooch and snog with a loved one is to act on one's natural disposition which, coming from God, is godly, but perhaps he pursues no consummation beyond that. It is in this sensuous niche that many a poem nests, such as a characteristically descriptive scene in which the speaker sits by the fire with his 'child-lover' on his lap and notices that *'one adventurous foot to be more free / Has slipped its sheath, and now from heel to toe / Vibrates within the hollow of my knee.'*[144]

Sometimes physical pleasure and spiritual love are enmeshed rather ambiguously: *'When Saints each other see / With chaste desire, / Hell will be verily / Less hot than heaven!'*,[145] and *'He that can see in Love impurity / In any form, or in the least degree— / Love, naked, shameless, wild—no saint is he, / But a low fool, or a cold-blooded sot.'*[146] In addition, to describe spiritual love Bradford not seldom borrows the language of physical love. There is

[142] 'To My Book', *Lays of Love and Life* (1916), p. 5.
[143] 'In Quest of Love', *In Quest of Love and Other Poems* (1914), p. 10
[144] 'Childhood and Age', ibid., p. 49.
[145] 'The Heat of Love', ibid., p. 54.
[146] 'Pure Love', ibid., p. 56.

repeated reference to the laying bare of the spirit, which creates an exalted bond: *'He laid his spirit bare—showed me the whole'.*[147]

Portrait of Young Boy on the Beach *(1898) by Denman Waldo Ross. The seaside town in Bradford's poetry is an idealised, dreamlike location.*

---

[147] 'Love Laughs at Time', *Passing the Love of Women and Other Poems* (1913), p. 39.

As regards the liberally used word 'love', the following observa-
tion of Bradford's may help clarify his take on that elusive con-
cept: 'The opposite to love is not hate—this is often only a dis-
guised form of love—but blank indifference.'[148] Love to him,
then, means difference: taking an interest, making a difference
to each other.[149] With this condition in place, the passionate
physical expression of love need not be shunned, but chasing
physical satisfaction for its own sake is to be frowned upon. He
seems to say as much where he specifies on the one hand that
desire *is not more bad or good / Than thirst or hunger*' and that
*'Woman is not my foe, nor carnal bliss: / Woman was made by
God; and clean desire / Is part of human nature'*, while on the
other hand he castigates 'low lust' and 'low passion' that over-
whelm friendship, honour and love.[150] Compare also: *'desire /
Without affection shrivels like a curse / The heart that harbours
its unholy fire.*'[151] And: *'Who loves the body only? Grind it small, /
Bring him the bloody mass—give him the whole. / Is he content?
Nay, when he has it all, / All is but naught without the informing
soul.*'[152] In his more abstentious moods, he shows himself to be
averse to the complicated ways in which sexual desire is resolved
on earth and pins his hopes on an afterlife where the whole busi-
ness will be sorted: *'I pondered on that perfect life where will /
Be neither sex nor marriage, and where Love, / Having no carnal
office to fulfil, / Will soar aloft'*.[153] And occasionally he hints that

---

[148] *Sermon Sketches for the Sundays of the Christian Year* (1907), p. 172.

[149] He also says Love assumes three forms, 'worthy all in their degrees',
from least high to highest: Desire, Fancy and Friendship. Lust, on the
other hand, pleases itself regardless of who may suffer and springs from
Hate – 'In Quest of Love', *In Quest of Love and Other Poems* (1914), p. 13.

[150] 'My Casus Belli', *Lays of Love and Life* (1916), p. 11.

[151] 'Chapter LIV: An Incurable Case', *Strangers and Pilgrims* (1929), p. 102.

[152] 'No Love Is Carnal', *Lays of Love and Life* (1916), p. 76.

[153] 'Fomes Peccati', *Passing the Love of Women and Other Poems* (1913),
p. 32. This well-constructed poem presents an ingenious parable of a
younger and older boy who experience the 'bliss of friendship pure'; the
older boy then comes across a pair of girls and there is sexual ten-

not everything he proclaims in his poetry should be taken as gospel: *'What! Must we kiss again? Well, be it so: / Exceptions, after all, but prove the rule— / Maybe at times (the world need never know!) / Keen eyes can wink, and wise men play the fool!'*[154]

Bradford's poetry books were advertised in the papers, review copies were sent out and the books were widely reviewed throughout Britain and Ireland, including in the most prominent papers and magazines such as *The Times, The Times Literary Supplement, The Athenæum, The Westminster Review, The Lady, The Scotsman, The Glasgow Herald, The Isle of Man Times, The Belfast News-Letter* and *The Cork Examiner*. What did the critics have to say about his unusual subject matter? By and large, they declared themselves well-pleased by his verse, noting its solid craftsmanship and approving of its bracing, cheery tone. A verdict such as that of *The Freeman's Journal* about *In Quest of Love and Other Poems* (1914) conveys the general sentiment: 'This is a well-printed, neatly-bound, little volume of verses, in which the charms of boyhood and youth are extolled in picturesque and melodious lines. The youths of various climes engage the author's attention. Besides the verses comprised in the poem giving a name to the collection there are other little verses expressive of phases of love and friendship, and all marked by liveliness, sympathy, a quick imagination, and a winning simplicity.'[155] It has

---

sion. The younger girl is distressed, but the older girl seeks to seduce him. The situation is defused when a bell tolls for Evensong. The poem bears out that sexual awareness comes with age but is also awakened by a confrontation between the sexes, whereas in a world without womankind boys would love each other in a pure, undefiled way. The attempt 'to associate sexual desire with women, whilst associating male love with purity and a greater spirituality', says Alderson (1998), 'was a particular strategy of many promoting same-sex love at this time' (p. 68).

[154] 'The Turning-Point', *Passing the Love of Women and Other Poems* (1913), p. 53.

[155] 'Current literature. Reviews of recent publications', *The Freeman's Journal*, 25 April 1914 (p. 5).

been argued that the written expression of same-sex love was deemed unobjectionable when presented in a Christian context[156] or as being free from the carnal desire that contaminated male-female relations.[157] Bradford certainly knew how to clothe boy love in religiously tinged ideals of chivalry, comradeship and the rejection of female enticement.

A related explanation of the generally benevolent reception his verse enjoyed centres on the argument that passions society could not conceive of would have been naively understood as expressing a non-sexual type of affection, 'a platonic love between man and boy, of a temporary and helpful nature – such as a scoutmaster might enjoy with his charges'.[158] The very concept of same-sex sexual attraction at the time was not, as it is now, an undisguised and ubiquitous cultural staple. Bradford's time was therefore more capable of chaste interpretations of homoerotic lyricism. In addition, there was the 'prevalence then of esteem for a classical education, which gave a certain air of scholarship and respect to aspects of homosexuality – so long as it was expressed in the rarefied world of poetry'.[159] This deference to classical learning is exemplified by a review that observed: 'Each of the forty or more of the poems deals with the form of love the

---

[156] Roden (2002), p. 235.

[157] 'Bradford's praise of the boy and his body did not involve any kind of conscious carnal desire and hence was purer than heterosexual relations, a superior kind of love since carnality was not deemed a possibility' – Hatt (2006), p. 90. This reading seems to have missed Bradford's 'Corpus Sanum', the last two stanzas of which read: *'Youth's tender body, clean and rosy white, / Is not that flesh corrupt we have to fight: / Its natural appetites are sane and right; / Its instinct true. // The mere word "carnal" shall not me affright; / Nor will I cease, in Puritans' despite, / To love the boyish body with the sprite, / And hymn it too'* – *The New Chivalry and Other Poems* (1918), p. 74.

[158] Webb (1988), p. 14. Cf. Young's (1994) description of 'Victorian society's' [sic] 'naïveté' as shown by *The Times*' 'benign approbation of the Rev. E. E. Bradford's series of sunny pederastic narrative fantasies' (p. 282).

[159] Webb (1988), p. 14.

copyright of which is attributed, more or less correctly, to Plato. Nearly every poet worthy of the name has devoted at least one poem to this'.[160] There was also the deference accorded to the clergy (a more exalted class in the era before pop culture stars), reflected in the author presenting himself to the world as 'Rev. E. E. Bradford', followed by the pertinent academic title.

While much Uranian verse may thus have been interpreted as passionate but chaste 'rhetoric of manliness and chivalric patriotism',[161] as safely Platonic or as a nostalgic celebration of boyhood, it would stretch credulity to argue that a verse like 'Free Love', which helpfully distinguishes lovers of lads from lovers of women,[162] or many other of Bradford's more assertive divulgences, could have been understood as free from sexual desire, whether or not acted upon. An alternative hypothesis is that the ranks of literary critics, or even society more generally, harboured considerably more broad-mindedness than Bradford's time is typically given credit for. But then, the modern view of pre-gay-rights-Britain as a time of uniform prudery, repression and narrow-mindedness is fed in part by a drive to contrast it with our own time, which imagines itself to be infinitely more compassionate, enlightened and emancipated with regard to sexual matters. In fact, the extreme taboo on age-discrepant friendship and sex – whether homosexual or heterosexual – where one of the parties is below a given 'age of consent' is a distinctly modern, historically aberrant taboo that should not be assumed for Bradford's time. The primary question therefore is how (if at all) his contemporaries reacted to the fact of his *homosexuality*, whereas the age discrepancy in his desire – its *pederastic* quality

---

[160] Vivian Carter, 'Thoughts on Things Read', *The Bystander*, 2 April 1913, p. 42.
[161] Roden (2002), p. 235.
[162] The first stanza reads: '*A lover of woman must learn to be / Content with one, and leave the rest; / But a lover of lads can do like me – / Make love to a hundred equally / And still love one the best.*' – In Quest of Love and Other Poems (1914), p. 43.

– is a secondary consideration at best.[163] If anything, pederasty was understood, justly, as the standard form of cultural expression of homosexuality down the ages.

It further bears keeping in mind that Bradford did not publish his poetry in the Victorian era, which the Uranian school is typically associated with, but between 1908 and 1930: the late Edwardian era, the time of the Great War and the first half of the interwar period. The Edwardian era, compared to the Victorian, was less conservative, more morally permissive and marked by a greater assertion of rights by the working class, women, ethnic minorities, homosexuals and other disadvantaged groups.[164] 'How the world wags! Fifteen years ago, or less, Dr. Bradford would probably have found himself hunted out of England for publishing this volume—that is, if any publisher might anywhere have been induced to risk his business on it', wrote *The New Age* on the appearance of *In Quest of Love and Other Poems* (1914).[165] Liberalising tendencies persisted in the war years and were further developed in the nineteen-twenties.[166] The titillating capers of the socialites referred to as the Bright Young Things, for whom the decade is famous in England, were eagerly covered by the

---

[163] Cf. the discussion of the difference in this respect between Bradford's time and the post-WWII West in Geoghegan (2011), pp. 69-71.

[164] Referencing a trend of sexual liberation and a greater understanding of 'the various kinks and quirks' of people's sex life through increased scientific interest, historian John Jacob Woolf characterises the Edwardians as 'a bit more sexy than we might like to think' (in the *HistoryExtra* podcast episode 'The Edwardians: everything you wanted to know', 19 June 2022).

[165] *The New Age*, no. 1128, 23 April 1914, p. 790.

[166] 'Homosexuals, like many others, would benefit from the lax atmosphere in Europe in the wake of the war. In the countries on the winning side, it was a time for optimism and making hay while the sun shined; after the suffering and privations, people wanted to laugh and have a good time, and were readier to tolerate the expression of sexual peccadilloes' – Tamagne (2006), p. 13.

press. A similar development took place elsewhere in Europe and in the United States, with terms like the Roaring Twenties, *les années folles* and *die Goldene Zwanziger* all giving a taste of the period's idiosyncrasy. By the following decade, attitudes were hardening again,[167] and the prosecution of homosexual sex intensified in England.[168] The changing fortunes in England in this regard ran parallel to – though they were less extreme than – the relative freedom of Germany's Weimar period versus the Nazis' consolidation of power in the early nineteen-thirties. These societal developments may help explain why Bradford resolved to go public with boy-love poetry, why he had it published when he did, and why he found a willing publisher and an accepting readership. Even with all this, it's still remarkable that he apparently experienced no obstruction from the church hierarchy. As anthologist Paul Webb notes: 'it seems incredible to a modern reader that Bradford's bishop should have let him publish such verse'.[169]

Reviewers of Bradford's day did sometimes let on that they were perfectly clear that his poetry's raison d'être lay in his sexual attraction to boys. One review explains: 'Mr. Bradford is a lover of boys and he has sought for his inspiration amongst them with great success. He exalts the love of man and man or man and boy over that of man and woman'.[170] Such lines are neither naive nor evasive, and perhaps our present age struggles to accept that reviewers in Bradford's day could have both understood and accepted his boy love because the modern age sees boy love as practically the most infamous crime imaginable. Surely Brad-

---

[167] 'if, in the mid-Twenties, one might have believed there had been a long-term triumph for the forces of progress, it was clear by 1931-1933 that the embryonic shift was not supported by a real desire for change nor by a large-scale acceptance of modern values' – ibid., p. 259.
[168] Ibid., p. 309.
[169] Webb (27 February 1988), p. 15.
[170] *The Poetry Review: Volume XIV* (Galloway Kyle (ed.), 1923, United Kingdom: Poetry Society), reviewing *Ralph Rawdon: A Story in Verse* (1922).

ford's contemporaries would have seen it that way too, the reasoning goes, if only they hadn't been fooled into thinking he was expressing Platonic camaraderie and Christian chivalry. In fact, his daring was admired: 'Apart from [his work's] literary merit, the courage and honesty with which he faces different questions are worthy of all admiration.'[171] When an occasional expression of reservation turns up, it is mildly worded, as though unwilling to make a to-do. Take this extract from a review of *The New Chivalry and Other Poems* (1918): 'to find a succession of poems to "Hilary," "Frederick," "Frank," "Will," and others is not common in English verse. We imagine the boys themselves, if they exist, looking rather red and sheepish. We think on the whole we prefer the ardent robust lustiness of the seventeenth century lyrists.'[172] Elsewhere, the same collection is described matter-of-factly as 'a fresh setting forth, from the pen of the Rev. E. E. Bradford, of his creed of boy-love in preference to the love of women'; the article then signals the appearance of another writer's collection of poems about children, which it says has an 'infinitely more natural attitude towards young life'.[173] A review of *Passing the Love of Women and Other Poems* (1913), while conceding that 'the verses on individual boys (bathing or otherwise) have occasional charm', adds: 'They are, however, too often spoilt by a certain smarminess of manner and by conclusion with a false platitude. As for his point of view, he might open his eyes if we told him all we thought about it.'[174]

Yet another review of *The New Chivalry* seems to employ a different strategy by quoting only some anaemic lines unrelated to

---

[171] From *Literary World*, cited in *The Romance of Youth and Other Poems* (1920), p. 90.
[172] 'The New Chivalry and other Poems', *The Educational Times and Journal of the College of Preceptors*, vol. 71, part 1, 1919, p. 144.
[173] 'A Group of Autumn Poets', *The Birmingham Post*, 20 September 1918, p. 3.
[174] In Harold Monro (ed.) (1913), *Poetry and Drama. Volume I: 1913*, London: The Poetry Bookshop, p. 256.

boy love.[175] All this creates the impression that even if reviewers were sometimes embarrassed or put off, they had no stomach for taking on a subject so perplexing to them and preferred to gloss over it rather than taking public issue with it. Those who privately disliked a frank poem could shake their head, move on to a poem expressing a chaster sentiment, then nod and prefer to keep the latter in mind when writing their review. One can even imagine the author and his reviewers together keeping up a dance of strategic ambiguity.[176] And those pundits who shared or sympathised with Bradford's Uranian outlook could nod knowingly about both types of poem and help the cause along with an appreciative review.[177]

In sum: Bradford's attraction to boys and boyhood, and his antipathy to female sexuality, speak so clearly and persistently throughout his work that, even if one wanted to argue that the times were more naive, and even though Bradford emphasised the spiritual and pure ends of boy love, it cannot be maintained that gullible, chaste interpretations were what allowed his poetry to receive an overwhelmingly positive press across mainstream publications. In view also of internal evidence from the reviews and of liberalising tendencies after the Victorian era, the conclusion must be that, at least among the literati, boy love in early-20th-century Britain was viewed with a measure of benevolence and toleration that in the latter decades of that century was to

---

[175] 'The New Chivalry and Other Poems', *The Belfast News-Letter*, 3 January 1919, p. 6.

[176] This view – the opposite of the notion that Bradford harvested such affable reviews because of the reviewers' naiveté – is espoused by Parsons (1988): 'he succeeded in getting the press to enter into a conspiracy of polite silence as to the obvious tendency of his verses' (p. 293).

[177] d'Arch Smith (2001) observes that Bradford's verse 'had a certain cachet in undergraduate circles disposed to titter at affections still enduring, if they looked into their hearts, from the tuckshop *Schwärmerei* of a public-school past' (p. 4).

dissipate completely in Western society and, as a direct result, in much of the rest of the world.

5   *Sharing a pew on Parnassus: Bradford among his fellow poets*

A window on the seventy-five-year-old Bradford's life and thought is provided by the aforementioned visit by John Betjeman, the later Poet Laureate, then a young man of twenty-nine with a single poetry collection under his belt. Bradford united a range of qualities that attracted Betjeman's interest: he was a lesser-known poet, a boy lover (Betjeman was himself bisexual and wrote several sympathetic poems about boy lovers[178]), a churchman (Betjeman was fond of church architecture and ritual) and, last but not least, an eccentric. Betjeman spent the afternoon and evening of Sunday 8 December 1935 with Bradford at Nordelph and wrote about the day in his private journal.[179] A fire was going in the vicarage, which had pictures everywhere, including a reproduction of *The Princes in the Tower* by John Everett Millais ('*the luckless twain / King Edward and young York, as wan almost / As their white roses, sought and sought in vain / A single faithful friend*'[180]). There were also reproductions of paintings by Henry Scott Tuke, the Falmouth painter of bathing boys who was connected socially with the Uranian writers. The following lines by Bradford capture a quintessential scene by Tuke: '*The elder, Gilbert, poised with lifted hands, / Prepared to dive, while Barney rowed the boat. / A morning mist lay over sea and sands, / And now the sun shone through, from feet to throat / The boy's bare form was flushed with rosy light. / His hair was fair, and the unclouded blue / Of childlike*

---

[178] E.g., 'The Arrest of Oscar Wilde at the Cadogan Hotel', 'Monody on the Death of a Platonist Bank Clerk' and the impressive 'Shattered Image', in Betjeman (2006).
[179] Cited in Hillier (2002), pp. 62-3.
[180] 'The Romance of Youth', *The Romance of Youth and Other Poems* (1920), p. 4.

eyes was starred with sparkles bright.[181] One can imagine Bradford sitting in his study on a typical day, the sanctified silence of the large house only enhanced by the crackling fire in the hearth and the angry Fenland wind at the windows, poring over his verse singing the divine beauty of boys as the housemaid clears the tea things.

Our Jack (1886) by Henry Scott Tuke, depicting Tuke's friend Jack Rolling. Bradford hung his vicarage with reproductions of Tuke's paintings and wrote a poem, "Our Jack", about a dependable fisherboy. The quotation marks are Bradford's and suggest a reference to Tuke's painting.

---

[181] 'Chapter III: Met in Mist', *Boyhood* (1930), p. 4.

Not that the atmosphere in the vicarage would typically have been forbidding and the silence stony: Betjeman describes Bradford as a 'saintly and sweet little man' with a high voice, like Cottam's, who talked a lot and very fast. He looked frail and moved around in a quiet, hurried fashion. Betjeman thought he had an obvious cataract coming on. Either during the visit or some time before, Bradford knocked over the fire screen and broke it, but – as Betjeman later wrote in his journal – he refused to admit he was 'failing'. He still walked everywhere and claimed to walk sixteen miles on some days. Only two years before, he'd run three miles when late for a funeral. Having no car himself, he was thrilled at the sight of one. He kept press cuttings and articles, all 'very neatly docketed'.[182] Betjeman attended the church service: the red altar was draped with black cloths, and all candles were lighted. Bradford played the organ very well while a handsome little fellow pumped the instrument, and he preached an abstruse and clever sermon on the certainty of God. He explained to Betjeman that he gave children a penny for attending church, keeping the pennies for this purpose in little boxes in his desk drawer. (A penny used to buy you a copy of *The Boy's Own Paper*, but the price had gone up to a shilling by the 1930s.)[183]

---

[182] Betjeman's remark that Bradford had neatly docketed press cuttings and articles, along with Bradford's own comment that he had 'kept a little daily account of my spare moments for years, and I have found this such a help in avoiding waste of time' (*Sermon Sketches for the Sundays of the Christian Year*, p. 264), conveys the impression of a meticulous, methodical man.

[183] On church attendance by children, Bradford wrote: 'Take the young and uncorrupted boy to church. Probably he will be bored. Then this shows that it is not natural for children to go to church. Let him wander freely in the fields and woods, and hold high communion with Nature. When he grows older he may appreciate a visit to a museum or an art gallery. Leave him alone. Let him develop his nature freely. Let there be no painful system of repression, no dwarfing of part of his character.' – *Sermon Sketches for the Sundays of the Christian Year* (1907), p. 195.

Whereas earlier in life Bradford had been an Anglo-Catholic, no doubt inclined that way as a result of his Oxford education, he had since moved towards Modernism, although he continued to appreciate ritual.[184] According to Betjeman, Bradford's friendship with Cottam cooled because the latter remained Anglo-Catholic. Bradford told Betjeman he was working on a poem about the love of a Modernist boy for an Anglo-Catholic boy; in the poem, the Modernist boy's convictions triumphed.[185] Modernism, or Liberal Christianity, admitted modern biblical criticism and accepted Darwinian evolution.[186] The view that the Bible writers were fallible in their scientific knowledge is borne out in the verse novel *The Tree of Knowledge*, which expresses disapproval of 'the bibliolater'.[187] Keenly aware of the scientific discoveries and debates of his time, Bradford reconciled science and religion: '*When first he found he was evolved / From lower life, man thought he solved / The riddle of the universe / Without a God. We do not nurse / Such flattering illusions now. / What we have learnt is only how / God works His will. It seems that He / Must gain His ends by means as we.*'[188]

In matters of religion as well as love, the self-willed Bradford was happy to embrace unconventional views. This leads to some interesting departures from mainstream Christianity, as when he

[184] A poem such as 'The Abbey' (*Sonnets Songs & Ballads*, pp. 77-8) is an ode to the joys of church ritual.
[185] Hillier (1988), p. 177.
[186] Bradford and Betjeman discussed the evolutionary biologist Julian Huxley and the physicists Arthur Eddington and James Jeans, and Bradford wrote: 'Whether Revelation, as seems possible in the light of the Evolution theory, comes by degrees as man is prepared to receive it, or as we used to fancy in a series of infallible books that were guaranteed free from inaccuracies even in history and geography, is a question which we can leave to the experts' – *Sermon Sketches for the Sundays of the Christian Year* (1907), p. 74.
[187] *The Tree of Knowledge* (1925), pp. 50-2; 55-9; 64-5; 66-71.
[188] Ibid., 'Canto XXXVII: The Deity', p. 71.

explains: *'Well may we wonder why the Lord created / Man with free will and feeble as he is! / But did He do so? Is this even stated / In Genesis? // There, we are told, God "shaped" at the beginning / What might have been from all eternity.'*[189] Or: *'What if in Babylon men called Him Bel, / Apis in Egypt, Jupiter in Rome? / God was, is, will be, One Immutable.'*[190] Modernist Christianity was also social-justice-oriented. While his views on women were decidedly retrograde and his feelings about other cultures, nationalities and ethnicities were a mixed bag,[191] he had a social-justice streak, opposing drinking, gambling,[192] cruelty to animals, classism and the exploitation of labourers. With regard to the issue of social class, in the poem 'Medieval Oxford' he defends his university's record: *'And to this day, I'm proud to say, my dear old* alma mater */ Cares little if you're rich or poor, or who may be your* pater!'[193] In 'A Gentleman' he proclaims: *'Gentlemen*

---

[189] 'The Kingdom Within You', *The Kingdom Within You and Other Poems* (1927), p. 3.

[190] Ibid., p. 14.

[191] As a Christian he believed the Jews to be 'in darkness' for having rejected Christ (*Sermon Sketches for the Sundays of the Christian Year*, p. 214). Scattered mentions of the Jews are generally less than flattering, if vague, e.g. *'The Church of old protected Jews, / As men keep bees for honey; / She said, "If they our faith refuse, / Need we refuse their money?"'* – 'Canto XXXII: The Roman Fold', *The Tree of Knowledge*, p. 61. The poem 'Saint Hugh of Lincoln' (*Sonnets Songs & Ballads*, p. 107) repeats the libel, perhaps still generally assumed true at the time, that Little Hugh was killed by the Jews. Elsewhere, Bradford lays into the boast of some Englishmen that they are superior to other European nations (*Sermon Sketches for the Sundays of the Christian Year*, pp. 218-22).

[192] Several of Bradford's poems hold forth on the vices of alcohol and gambling. In a letter to *Christian World* he put gambling, including the football pools, on a par with theft ('Morality of Gambling', *Lynn Advertiser*, 4 February 1938, p. 9). He further wrote: 'Teetotalers, people who hate cruelty to animals, all religious professors who have any definite creed at all, are almost sure at times to appear in a comic light' – *Sermon Sketches for the Sundays of the Christian Year*, p. 44.

[193] *Sonnets Songs & Ballads* (1908), p. 64.

may gentle be / In nothing but in pedigree: / Whether of high or low degree / The gentle man's the man for me. [194] This is reiterated in *The True Aristocracy*: *'In future aristocracy / Will not depend on pedigree; / Wealth will not win gentility, / Nor title-deeds nobility.'* [195] For this verse novel Bradford may have been inspired by William Paine's *A New Aristocracy of Comradeship* (1920), which expounds on friendship – the code word at the time for not just friendship but also love and sexual relationships – between men and working boys. [196] Much has been written about the oft-encountered dyad, in Uranian literature and in practice, of the upper-class intellectual and his younger partner from a humbler milieu. At the end of the day, it is logical that those with the education and leisure to produce literature were often drawn *from* the upper classes and drawn *to* practical opportunities to bond with the working class. Adult labourers also aroused Bradford's pity, and he can suddenly sound political: *'See that this British soil be wholly freed / From landlord's lust of gold and farmer's greed, / And given to men!'* [197]

Bradford told Betjeman that his last boyfriend was called 'Edmund [?Edward] Monson' (this is how Betjeman later wrote it down in his journal), but that he had not had a boyfriend for thirty years. [198] He thought the 'laws against sexuality' wicked, cruel and out of date. He declared himself in favour of birth control and said that logically, onanism was a must and should be permitted in public schools. He'd read Freud, but didn't believe him. The other day he'd had a dream: a big boy asked him to go to a house in Torquay, his place of birth. He knew he was to go

---

[194] *Lays of Love and Life* (1916), p. 85.
[195] 'Chapter V: The Great and the Chief', *The True Aristocracy* (1923), p. 8.
[196] d'Arch Smith (1970), p. 89.
[197] 'A Cry from the Fens', *Sonnets Songs & Ballads* (1908), p. 74.
[198] I.e., Edmund or Edward Monson was his boyfriend – of whatever description, sexual or nonsexual – about 1905, the year in which Bradford moved from Eton to Upwell.

there for a bad purpose. He saw the house and experienced noth-
ing, but felt as though he were a boy of eight again. He told
Betjeman the Queen had once asked him for an autograph of one
of his books, and reflected: "I wonder why she wanted it. Perhaps
for the Prince of Wales. I have often thought he may be a
Platonist." The Queen in question would have been Queen Con-
sort Mary of Teck, wife of George V. The Prince of Wales whom
Bradford suspected of being a 'Platonist' was their womanising
son Edward, who would rule briefly in 1936 but would abdicate
the throne in order to marry the divorcee Wallis Simpson. Betje-
man says Bradford used the term 'Platonist' a good bit on the day
of the visit, and Betjeman himself used it in the title of his poem
'Monody on the Death of a Platonist Bank Clerk'. A character in
Bradford's verse novel *Boyhood* defines a Platonist as *'A man with
more capacity / For friendship than for love'*.[199] When Bradford's
poetry was called Platonic, for instance in reviews, this may not
always have referred to nonsexual love, but may at times have
been a euphemism for same-sex sexual attraction.[200] The story
about the Queen's request prompted Betjeman to jot down in his
journal: 'Obviously a joke played on him poor old thing.'

This little comment by Betjeman is emblematic of a wider cir-
cumstance Bradford was presumably unaware of: the subject
matter of his verse, combined with the melodramatic quality of
some of it and the daintily worded commendations his work

---

[199] 'Chapter XXXV: Amnon', *Boyhood* (1930), p. 61.
[200] An example of the use of 'Platonic Love' as code for male-male (or
perhaps specifically man-boy) attraction and relations is furnished by the
Wilde apologist Wilfrid Morley Leadman (1881–1953), who wrote to
Bradford having read *The True Aristocracy* (1923): 'I am with you heart
and soul in your glorious crusade for winning over the plain man to an
understanding of Platonic Love' – d'Arch Smith (2017), p. 397. Bradford's
sonnet 'Platonic Love' defines such love both in terms of its distinctness
from the love of women and in terms of it involving a 'passion passion-
less', i.e. spiritual rapture rather than carnal desire – *Passing the Love of
Women and Other Poems* (1913), p. 12.

received in newspaper reviews, was a source of great hilarity to Betjeman and his friends, including the poet Wystan Hugh Auden and the archaeologist Stuart Piggott.[201] Betjeman was irresistibly drawn to the camp and risqué quality of Bradford's outspoken boy-love poetry,[202] knew several of his poems by heart (as did Piggott) and expressed the hope that more readers would discover him. In Betjeman's own words: 'Wystan and I much enjoyed discovering unknown poets, preferably of the last century and the Edwardian age and reading out our discoveries to each other. This was how we stumbled on the works of the Reverend Doctor E. E. Bradford, DD, whose lyrics, innocent and touching about the love of 'lads', as boys were so often called by scoutmasters in those days, used to bring us uncontrollable mirth.'[203] Betjeman and Auden were fascinated by Cottam for similar reasons, and the two went to hear Cottam celebrate sung mass in his parish of Wootton, Berkshire.[204] To more than a few, whether or not put on their trail by Betjeman, these two clergymen's spirited defence of something so outlandish must have made them seem zany and quixotic.[205] Indeed, Bradford was – and is – not quite taken seriously by all. The novelist Dorothy L. Sayers, whose father was the rector of the parish of Christchurch, Cambridgeshire near Nordelph, called him 'an entertaining little

---

[201] Hillier (1988), pp. 176-7; Hillier (2002), pp. 14 & 190.

[202] Hillier (2002), pp. 14, 191 & 627. Betjeman recalled the following lines in which Bradford went over the top sentimentally: '*Once a schoolboy newly come, / Timid, frail, and friendless, / Feared to face a "footer scrum." / Oh, the taunts were endless! // Presently he drew apart, / Soon they heard him crying: / With a penknife in his heart / Home they brought him dying.*' The two quatrains are from 'Canto XIV: An Errant Knight-Errant', *The Tree of Knowledge* (1925), p. 25, and amended in accordance with Bradford's original text.

[203] Green (1998), p. 485.

[204] Hillier (1988), p. 177.

[205] Cf. Bradford's rueful statement 'It is so easy to put a ridiculous light on the actions of any kind of enthusiasts', in *Sermon Sketches for the Sundays of the Christian Year* (1907), p. 44.

crank—and rather a dear'.[206] Paul Webb, while expressing strong admiration for Bradford, stresses the comic effect of his work: 'So over-the-top are his poems, however, that they will not offend any save the most prudish of readers; in fact they are often hilariously camp. One cannot understand why the editor of the *Penguin Book of Homosexual Verse* failed to include a single one, unless he feared the merriment that is inevitably aroused by a recitation of some of Bradford's gems.'[207]

When some modern critics dismiss Bradford and Cottam – or the Uranians in general – after discussing them cursorily, it can be hard to decide where the critique of their literary qualities ends and where the disgust at their sexuality begins. Just like Black Africans were considered to have been incapable of building as majestic a city as Great Zimbabwe, it seems some writers must be deemed inconsequential by dint of their sexual orientation. To cite a few examples: Noël Annan, in a letter in the *London Review of Books*, calls the verse of Bradford and other Uranians 'grotesquely comical', adding: 'The poetry of these paedophiles is atrocious.'[208] Graham Robb opines that '[t]he recurring characteristics of English 'boy-worship' are self-deception, trickery and bad poetry'.[209] Bevis Hillier refers to Bradford's 'ludicrous paedophilic poems'.[210] Matthew Harrison expresses himself more mildly but no less tellingly: 'It is hard to know what to make of it [Bradford's poetry] with our contemporary perspective, but the writer [d'Arch Smith] of the one recent book about this group of poets, the Uranians, is convinced that the worst crime they can be convicted of is writing bad poetry.'[211] In other words: given Bradford's subject matter, one thinks of (potential) crime

---

[206] d'Arch Smith (2001), p. 11.
[207] Webb (27 February 1988), p. 14.
[208] *London Review of Books*, vol. 4, no. 6, 1 April 1982.
[209] Robb (2003), p. 218.
[210] Hillier (2002), p. 190.
[211] Harrison (2005), p. 52.

first and foremost, in the light of which it's just as well, and un-surprising, that he can be dismissed as a bad poet.

Bradford's inclusion in anthologies of stuffed-owl poetry (ingenious but unintentionally funny versification), such as Parsons' *The Joy of Bad Verse* (1988), is probably not solely on the strength of his penchant for moralising and melodrama, but also due to the circumstance that an oeuvre built on the adoration of boys is seen as inherently ridiculous. Aside from this, taste is fickle. On Bradford's tearjerker 'His Mother Drinks', *The Dundee Advertiser* wrote that its 'terrible realism' was bound to 'move others than women to tears'.[212] Fast-forward to the late 20th century, and we find the poem included in the said anthology as well as in Petras and Petras' *Very Bad Poetry* (1997). In assessing comments on Bradford's poetry, or that of the Uranians in general, one should keep sight of the fact that many a commentator has only come across this poetry tangentially, in the course of research on a different subject. Some have read only snatches of Bradford's poems or are completely unfamiliar with his work, which has been hard to come by. Indeed, the *idée reçue* of Bradford as a bad poet across the board can only be maintained by not reading him.

In contrast with several later critics, Betjeman, while amused at Bradford's expense, also had a genuine appreciation for his work. This stands to reason: the tight, musical composition of Bradford's verse is akin to his own style. Any notion that he only chummed up with Bradford the better to gloat over the eccentric pervert's preposterous poetry would bespeak a poor understanding of both men and their work. Lamenting that Bradford's poems never got into anthologies,[213] Betjeman included 'Paddy Maloy' in his selection for *The Saturday Book* annual miscellany of 1965.[214] Another admirer was the Scottish poet Hugh MacDiarmid,

---

[212] Cited in *Lays of Love and Life* (1916), p. 165.

[213] Taylor-Martin (1983), p. 79.

[214] Betjeman (1965). The poem is from *Sonnets Songs & Ballads* (1908), p. 111.

who described Bradford's work as being 'full of direct grappling with the problems of the age, hard thinking, common sense, plain statement, no flowers, and no monkey tricks; virile, useful', and declared: 'Many of our 'leading poets' would be greatly astonished if they could foresee how small they will look in comparison to Dr. Bradford'.[215]

The poet John Betjeman, here shown top centre at Marlborough College aged about sixteen, sought to popularise Bradford's poetry.

A reference to Bradford made its way into a poem by Betjeman, or at least into a footnote to it. 'A Shropshire Lad' – the title a

---

[215] In an article on 'Recent Poetry' in *The New Age*, as cited in *Strangers and Pilgrims* (1929), pp. 120-1.

wink to A. E. Housman's famous collection, but the poem itself a tribute, characteristically accomplished, to the drowned Shropshire stunt swimmer Matthew Webb – opens with the line 'The gas was on in the Institute'. The footnote clarifies that this was inspired by a line in Bradford's novel in verse *Boyhood*: 'The Institute was radiant with gas'.[216] As the opening line of Betjeman's poem is a droll one and hardly material to the subject of the poem, the arcane reference to Bradford appears intended as a mild dig. However, Betjeman wrote to him saying that he liked *Boyhood* perhaps best of all of Bradford's poetry books.[217] Auden, for his part, gave Bradford and Cottam a cameo appearance in his long poem 'Letter to Lord Byron'. The poem expresses regret that light verse has gone out of fashion and goes on to say: *'Parnassus after all is not a mountain, / Reserved for A.1. climbers such as you; / It's got a park, it's got a public fountain. / The most I ask is leave to share a pew / With Bradford or with Cottam, that will do'.*[218] Light verse is not the first genre that comes to mind when thinking of Bradford's and Cottam's poetry – they don't as a rule set out to make their point through humour, though Bradford is often witty enough and his poems have the jollity of songs.[219] Auden, then, seems to be classing them as minor poets

---

[216] 'Chapter XIX: A Small Great Man', *Boyhood* (1930), p. 32.

[217] d'Arch Smith (2017), p. 399.

[218] Auden's 'Letter to Lord Byron' was first published in *Letters from Iceland* (1937), a prose and verse collection co-authored by Auden and Louis MacNeice; Betjeman's 'A Shropshire Lad' was first published in *Old Lights for New Chancels* (1940).

[219] Eglinton (1964) says a 'light touch' is 'seldom found among the Calamites' (p. 386). (Calamites is his term, originally Algernon Charles Swinburne's [Mader, 2013, p. 412], for the Uranians; the latter term was subsequently popularised through d'Arch Smith's study *Love in Earnest*.) Bradford expresses black humour in 'The Humour of Heaven', in which a sick man speaks: *'"Why this ado? / Heaven has a sense of humour! / What's a cancer or a tumour / To a man about to be / Set by death for ever free?" / Then he turned upon his side, / Laughing choked, and choking died'* – In Quest of Love and Other Poems (1914), p. 100.

irrespective of their poetic style. It has been argued that Auden implies Bradford and Cottam 'are secondary not just in the quality of their writing but in their self-construction as members of a gay poetic lineage'.[220] Bradford has at times been given short shrift by curators of the lineage, such as when the reader's companion *The Gay & Lesbian Literary Heritage* deemed his poetry 'of interest for only thematic rather than aesthetic and qualitative reasons'.[221]

If Bradford's and Cottam's poetic efforts were not always rated top-class, they themselves did not necessarily fawn on each other's productions. Cottam, his friend's most exacting critic, not to say a cantankerous and fault-finding one, didn't pull punches in handwritten comments in his copies of Bradford's books. As an example, in *Ralph Rawdon: A Story in Verse* (1922), he struck out all of Chapter V in Book V with visibly angry thick pencil strokes, adding: 'I seem to have written I find this "simply bull". It is utter bosh'. His copy of *The True Aristocracy* (1923) includes a detailed critique of a single unfortunate word choice of Bradford's, ending on the triumphant conclusion: 'E. E. B. has made one of his characteristic blunders'.[222] They also corresponded with each other about such textual matters. Bradford wrote to Cottam about the latter's sole volume of poetry, *Cameos of Boyhood and Other Poems* (1930): 'I am perfectly amazed and delighted [...] I nearly always find books of verse unreadably dull. Yours is a complete exception'.[223] In 1935, however, he told Betjeman he thought Cottam was no poet and was going mad. Betjeman and Auden also thought Cottam in his later years was going mad and would 'have to be taken away soon'.[224]

---

[220] Trousdale (2018), p. 160.
[221] Summers (2013).
[222] d'Arch Smith (1970), Plate 21 facing p. 168.
[223] Ibid., p. 123.
[224] Hillier (2002), p. 63.

Betjeman was not the only person to travel to Nordelph to experience Bradford for himself. Timothy d'Arch Smith, biographer and bibliographer of the Uranians, tells an anecdote about an unnamed lifelong Bradford fan who, like Betjeman, had discovered the poet in his university days. As an undergraduate, this fan once bicycled over from Cambridge to Nordelph, where he was given a tour of the church. At the end of an agreeable visit, Bradford expressed the hope that the young man would come again and bring along a pal. The young man duly visited again later in the term with a college friend. Bradford, when he found an opportunity, remarked discreetly to his second-time visitor: "I like your pal, but I was expecting him to be a... rather younger fellow."[225]

When Betjeman visited Bradford, it had been five years since the publication of Bradford's last book, *Boyhood*. d'Arch Smith heard it said much later that the writer Beverley Nichols had attacked this book in a review for being indecent; d'Arch Smith was unable to trace such a review. The denunciation allegedly upset Bradford to such a degree that he never published another word.[226] One can speculate about other reasons that may have underlain the lack of literary output in the last fourteen years of his life: perhaps he'd said all he wanted to say (but this is unlikely, as he told Betjeman he was working on a poem), he'd grown less ardent with advancing age, writing was becoming more difficult (Betjeman, after all, said his eyesight was deteriorating) or the sales of his books had declined. As he commented in a letter to the writer Leonard Henry Green: 'Only about one man in a hundred is interested in my subject.'[227] But this would

---

[225] d'Arch Smith (2001), p. 5.

[226] Ibid., p. 6.

[227] Letters from Bradford to Leonard Henry Green, Nordelph, 1922, quoted in deHartington (1972), p. 7. In the same letter, incidentally, Bradford gave voice to his characteristic optimism: 'I find many Bishops and dignitaries are not quite so narrow as one may think.'

hardly explain why eleven previous collections had apparently not suffered from a discouraging lack of interest, or not enough to cause him to hang his harp upon the willows. It is even conceivable that he or his publisher sensed that the times had become less auspicious for countercultural poetry: as discussed above, relative to the twenties, the thirties were a less forgiving decade with regard to alternative sexualities.

In view of his extensive travels, his curacies near London as well as a poem such as 'Piccadilly' (Piccadilly Circus was well-known as a spot where one could loiter and meet boys),[228] it is likely that Bradford found himself in the capital more than a few times and had opportunity there to socialise with other Uranians. If he was as talkative on paper as he was in person, he must also have sent out a fair amount of letters. He must be counted among the later Uranians, not with regard to his year of birth but with regard to the fact that most of his poetry books appeared in the nineteen-tens and nineteen-twenties. d'Arch Smith identifies an upsurge of Uranian writings between 1858, when the collection of verse *Ionica* by William Johnson – later William Johnson Cory – came out, and 1930, the year of publication of the only poetry collection by Cottam to appear in his lifetime as well as of Bradford's final offering.[229]

Several of Bradford's friends and acquaintances moved in Uranian literary and activist circles, such as Edward Carpenter (whose work expressed his ideas about 'spiritual democracy' – love as the shatterer of class divisions – under the influence of Walt Whitman), George Cecil Ives (founder of the secret homosexual society, the Order of Chaeronea), Leonard Henry Green

---

[228] d'Arch Smith (2001) says that 'Bradford's being much of a jumper-into-bedder is not a speculation to be seriously entertained' (p. 6). While Bradford's poetry suggests that he aspired to loftier ideals than casual lust, it suggests equally that he was far from a vestal virgin who sublimated his desires entirely into religion and poetry.
[229] d'Arch Smith (1970), p. 1.

(who in turn was a close friend of T. E. Lawrence – yes, of Arabia), John Leslie Barford (who wrote poetry under the pseudonym Philebus and whom Bradford called an 'excellent fellow, if a little mad'[230]) and Horatio Robert Forbes Brown (the historian of Venice and biographer of John Addington Symonds).[231] On the other hand, the little-known poetess Octavia Gregory from Parkstone, Dorset, who dedicated her volume *Dreams of Arcady* (1913) to Bradford,[232] is unlikely to have had the least connection with things Uranian. Bradford's poetry books further led to letters to him from, among others, author Lionel Birch, poet Charles Kains Jackson, author John Masefield (Poet Laureate from 1930 to 1967), classical scholar Gilbert Murray, poet John Gambril Nicholson and anthologist Edward Mark Slocum.[233] This American, through his correspondence and his groundbreaking poetry anthology *Men and Boys* (1924), formed a link between the English Uranian poets and their American counterparts.[234] *Men and Boys* includes Bradford's poems 'Shy Love', 'When I Went A-Walking' and 'Alan', as well as his translations of poems by the Greek poets Anacreon, Pindar and Rhianus and the Roman poet Tibullus. Another glimpse of Bradford's ties with the Uranian world is afforded by his contribution of a sonnet, 'Friendship and Love', to *The Quorum. A Magazine of Friendship.* Launched in 1920, this boy-love magazine was, like its much earlier predecessor *The Chameleon*, fated to fold after a single issue. It was circulated as a specimen copy to the members of the British Society for the Study of Sex Psychology and had probably been produced by members of that same society and/or of the Order of Chaeronea.[235] d'Arch Smith in fact credits Bradford as one of the

---

[230] In a letter to Leonard Henry Green dated 25 January 1922 – d'Arch Smith (1970), pp. 146 & 160.
[231] Kaylor (2010), pp. 4 & 52.
[232] 'New Books', *Bournemouth Guardian*, 27 September 1913, p. 9.
[233] d'Arch Smith (2017), pp. 395-6.
[234] Mader (2013), pp. 380-1.
[235] d'Arch Smith (2001), p. 13.

founders of *The Quorum*.[236] The magazine seems to have been discontinued at the insistence of George Cecil Ives, who favoured secrecy and feared negative publicity.[237] Outside of Uranian circles, Bradford proved himself a joiner by becoming one of the vice-presidents of the (International) Institute of British Poetry, founded in 1916 'to commemorate the tercentenary of the death of Shakespeare and Cervantes and the centenary of the birth of Charlotte Brontë'.[238]

The Princes in the Tower *(1878) by John Everett Millais, a reproduction of which hung in Bradford's Nordelph vicarage*

---

[236] d'Arch Smith (1970), p. 140.
[237] d'Arch Smith (2001), pp. 14-5.
[238] 'Institute of British Poetry', *The Belfast News-Letter*, 21 February 1917, p. 3.

6 Late life and after life

In the year of Betjeman's visit to Nordelph, 1935, Bradford's sister Ada Bessie died and administration was granted to him; two years later his sister Rosa Kate died and probate was granted to him. He had evidently been on good terms with at least these family members. Curiously, they as well as their sister Ella Maria were all lifelong spinsters. Ada Bessie lived with her brother George Frank, a schoolmaster who never married, either. Of the seven Bradford siblings who reached adulthood, the only two to marry were Amelia Hembrew (Minnie) and Louis Henry, who like Edwin was a clergyman.[239] The 1939 England and Wales Register shows Bradford living with his sixty-year-old housekeeper Sarah Esther Beales. The outbreak of World War II must have been a terrible disappointment to him. He had shared in the idealism of the founding of the League of Nations after the Great War, referring to it as *'a pact of the peoples so wisely planned / That I trust it will end all strife!'*[240] In 1940, with the wartime blackout in force, he was fined nine shillings – and twenty shillings and sixpence in costs – for having allowed light to shine from the vicarage.[241] There was another incident: he 'was once apprehended at Denver [a village near Nordelph] on the river wall as being a suspect spy'.[242] This must have been in either of the wars, but could the elderly Bradford have been mistaken for a spy in his final years in the forties? At any rate, any spying he did undertake is unlikely to have been political in nature.

---

[239] Minnie married jeweller Charles Pickering Roberts; Louis Henry married Laura Gwendoline Blackwood, daughter of the 4th Baronet Blackwood.

[240] 'Resurrection', *The Romance of Youth and Other Poems* (1920), p. 81. Cf. the observation by Davidson (2022): 'That was a time when all the idealists' hopes, and all the politicians' cynicism, were poured into the new League of Nations' (p. 12).

[241] 'Petty Sessional Intelligence', *Lynn Advertiser*, 22 November 1940, p. 5.

[242] Communication from Jane Crapnell to Knott (2005).

Bradford continued to serve his community right up to the time of his death.[243] On 7 February 1944, the eighty-three-year-old poet died at the vicarage, the last surviving Bradford sibling. Cottam had preceded him in death by just under a year. Bradford was buried at Nordelph[244] and left his property, including personal copies of his poetry books, to his last housekeeper.[245, 246] The battered vicarage was demolished not long after his death, Bradford's attempt to recreate a Swiss lake next to it apparently having been the final nail in the building's coffin.[247] The church held out a good deal longer, but was cracked and unstable by the end of the century and was torn down in 2010 (that excellent stained-glass window noted by Pevsner was preserved).[248] Where once Edwin Emmanuel Bradford wrote his Uranian love lyrics and visions and rewarded Nordelph's children with pennies for coming to listen to the Holy Word, a housing development has since gone up known as Church Cottages. Coinciding with Bradford's death was the waning of the Uranian ideal, which was displaced and strategically demonised by a new, egalitarian, androphile gay rights movement that used the heterosexual marriage for a model.

Bradford's poetry encountered a highly engaged reading public in his lifetime. d'Arch Smith speaks of 'the chivalric ties of friendship that bound the Uranian poets together in their singing of a common theme and the enthusiasm and loyalty their readers

---

[243] E.g., he conducted a funeral service in November 1943 ('Mrs. M. L. Clark (Nordelph)', *Lynn Advertiser*, 5 November 1943, p. 2) and officiated at a wedding in December ('Mr. L. G. Ireland — Miss A. M. Secker', *Lynn Advertiser*, 3 December 1943, p. 4).

[244] 'Deaths', *Lynn Advertiser*, 11 February 1944, p. 1; 'Clergy's Tribute at Nordelph', ibid., 3 March 1944, p. 5.

[245] England & Wales, National Probate Calendar (Index of Wills and Administrations), 1858-1995.

[246] Communication from Jane Crapnell, grandniece of Sarah Esther Beales, to Knott (2005).

[247] Yelton (2009), p. 204.

[248] Knott (2005).

showed in buying their books, lending them to their friends, and addressing to the authors their letters of appreciation and encouragement.'[249] For all its fidelity, this loose network of writers and readers will not have been very large. At some point after 1934, Stuart Piggott, introduced to Bradford's poetry by Betjeman, found out through the latter that Kegan Paul had a lot of unsold stock of Bradford's books, which Piggott subsequently bought up.[250]

Since his death, Bradford has been discussed or anthologised occasionally, the most notable early treatments being Anderson and Sutherland's in 1961, Eglinton's in 1964 and d'Arch Smith's in 1970. A selection from his poetry edited by Webb was published in 1988 (*To Boys Unknown*), and he was featured in Kaylor's two-volume Uranian poetry and prose anthology of 2010, which built on d'Arch Smith's research.[251] Bradford's books were never reprinted; they are not cheap in the antiquarian market. His subject matter, his unique voice and his place among the Uranians will ensure that he continues to come to the attention of academics and select, happy readers.

In 2021 his alma mater, Exeter College, acquired the author's copies of his books.[252] These contain his abundant handwritten comments and revisions, including copied reviews and feedback

---

[249] d'Arch Smith (2017), p. 395.
[250] Hillier (2002), p. 14.
[251] Credit is also due to Barry Van-Asten for *Desire and Divinity: A Brief Biographical Sketch of Reverend Edwin Emmanuel Bradford (1860-1944)*, published on his blog at https://ghostblooms-van-asten.blogspot.com/2019/06/edwin-emmanuel-bradford.html on 15 June 2019. D. H. Mader (1948–2022) announced a thesis on Bradford and four other Christian boy-love poets (2013, p. 377), which seems to have remained unfinished and unpublished.
[252] Wood (2021).

from admirers and critics.[253] Some of his notes are in a private code, assessed by cryptology expert Klaus Schmeh as possibly being a self-invented combination of shorthand writing and ordinary letters.[254] It is an open question whether the art of cryptology will one day unlock the secrets contained in these notes. It seems likely this would shed new light not just on Bradford's life but on the wider Uranian world.

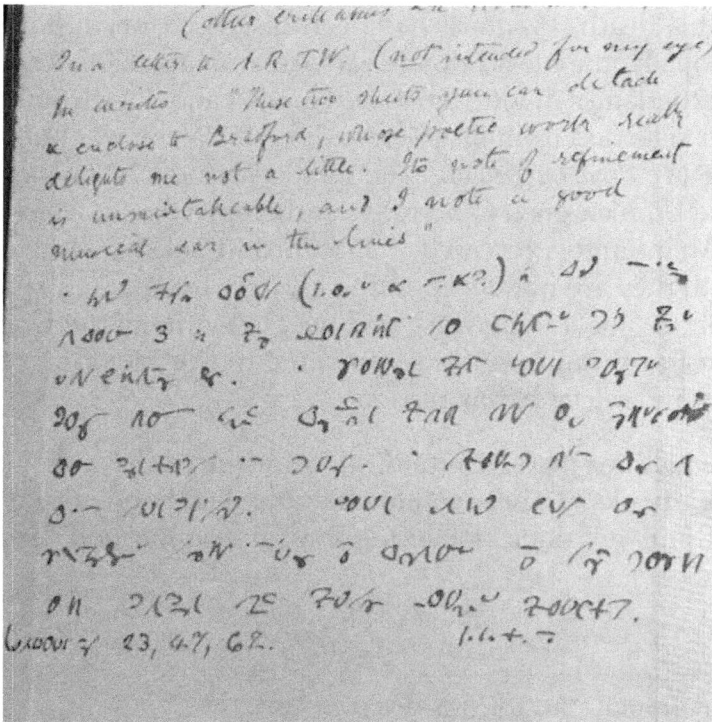

A sample of Bradford's encrypted notes awaiting decoding

---

[253] d'Arch Smith (2017) identifies four classes of handwritten additions by Bradford: emendations of his poems, coded notes, copied accolades from third parties for specific poems, and extracts – often lengthy – from letters to Bradford from fellow poets and other admirers (p. 395).
[254] Schmeh (2020).

References

Bradford's own works are listed separately under Publications by E. E. Bradford.

Alderson, David (1998), *Mansex Fine. Religion, Manliness and Imperialism in Nineteenth-Century British Culture*, Manchester and New York: Manchester University Press.

Aldrich, Robert and Garry Wotherspoon (eds.) (2001), *Who's Who in Gay & Lesbian History*, Oxon: Routledge. Entry on Bradford by David Hilliard.

Anderson, Patrick and Alistair Sutherland (eds.) (1961), *Eros: An Anthology of Friendship*, London: Anthony Blond.

Baker Esq., William (1851), *A Practical Compendium of the Recent Statuses, Cases, and Decisions Affecting the Office of Coroner*, London: Butterworths.

Betjeman, John (ed.) (1965), 'Poems of the Nineties chosen by John Betjeman', in John Hadfield (ed.) *The Saturday Book 25*, London: Hutchinson.

Betjeman, John (2006) (first published 1958), *Collected Poems*, London: John Murray.

d'Arch Smith, Timothy (1970), *Love in Earnest: Some Notes on the Lives and Writings of English 'Uranian' Poets from 1889 to 1930*. London: Routledge & Kegan Paul.

d'Arch Smith, Timothy (1987), *The Books of the Beast: Essays on Aleister Crowley, Montague Summers, Francis Barrett and Others*, Wellingborough: Crucible.

d'Arch Smith, Timothy (ed.) (2001), *The Quorum. A Magazine of Friendship. A facsimile edition with an Introduction by Timothy d'Arch Smith*, Asphodel Editions.

d'Arch Smith, Timothy (2017), 'The Poetry of E. E. Bradford: The Author's Own Copies', in *The Book Collector*, vol. 66, no. 2, pp. 391-9.

Davidson, Michael (2022) (first published 1969), *Some Boys*, London: Arcadian Dreams.

deHartington, Michael (1972), *English Homosexual Poetry of the Nineteenth and Twentieth Centuries*, catalogue no. 3.

Dynes, Wayne R. (ed.) (1990), *The Encyclopedia of Homosexuality*, New York: Garland.

Eglinton, J. Z. [Walter H. Breen] (1964), *Greek Love*, New York: Oliver Layton Press.

Foster, Joseph (1893), *Oxford Men and Their Colleges*, Oxford & London: James Parker & Co.

Geoghegan, Vincent (2011), *Socialism and Religion: Roads to Common Wealth*, London and New York: Routledge.

Green, Candida Lycett (ed.) (1998), *John Betjeman. Coming Home: An anthology of his prose 1920-1977*, London: Vintage.

Harrison, Matthew (2005), *An Anglican Adventure. The History of Saint George's Anglican Church, Paris*. Paris: Saint George's Anglican Church.

Hatt, Michael (2006), "A great sight': Henry Scott Tuke and his models', in Jane Desmarais, Martin Postle and William Vaughan (eds.), *Model and Supermodel: The Artist's Model in British Art and Culture*, Manchester and New York: Manchester University Press.

Hillier, Bevis (1988), *Young Betjeman*, London: John Murray.

Hillier, Bevis (2002), *John Betjeman: New Fame, New Love*, London: John Murray.

Kaylor, Michael Matthew (ed.) (2010), *Lad's Love: An anthology of Uranian poetry and prose. Volume I: John Leslie Barford to Edward Cracroft Lefroy*, Kansas City: Valancourt Books.

Knott, Simon (2005), 'Holy Trinity, Nordelph', at http://www.
norfolkchurches.co.uk/nordelph/nordelph.htm
(accessed March 2023).

Mader, D. H. (2013) (first published 2005), 'The Greek Mirror:
The Uranians and Their Use of Greece', in Beert C.
Verstraete and Vernon Provencal (eds.), *Same-Sex
Desire and Love in Greco-Roman Antiquity and in the
Classical Tradition of the West*, New York and London:
Routledge.

Norton, Rictor (1974, 1998), 'Blessed Are the *Puer* in Heart:
E. E. Bradford', on the website *Gay History &
Literature: Essays by Rictor Norton*, at https://rictornorton
.co.uk/bradford.htm (accessed March 2023).

Parsons, Nicholas T. (1988), *The Joy of Bad Verse*, London:
Collins.

Petras, Kathryn and Ross Petras (eds.) (1997), *Very Bad Poetry*,
New York: Vintage Books.

Quince, Travers Hartington (1919), *Bats, Boots, and Bathing
Togs*. Includes his Cornish translations of some of
Bradford's poems.

Reade, Brian (ed.) (2017) (first published 1970), *Sexual
Heretics: Male Homosexuality in English Literature
from 1850-1900*, Abingdon and New York: Routledge.

Rind, Bruce (2016) (first published 2013), 'Pederasty: An
Integration of Empirical, Historical, Sociological, Cross-
Cultural, Cross-Species, and Evolutionary Perspectives',
in Thomas K. Hubbard and Beert Verstraete (eds.),
*Censoring Sex Research: The Debate Over Male Intergen-
erational Relations*, London and New York: Routledge.

Rind, Bruce and Richard Yuill (2012), 'Hebephilia as Mental
Disorder? A Historical, Cross-Cultural, Sociological, Cross-
Species, Non-Clinical Empirical, and Evolutionary Review',
in *Archives of Sexual Behavior*, vol. 41, no. 4, pp. 797-829.

Robb, Graham (2003), *Strangers: Homosexual Love in the Nineteenth Century*, London: Picador.

Roden, Frederick S. (2002), *Same-Sex Desire in Victorian Religious Culture*, Basingstoke and New York: Palgrave Macmillan.

Schmeh, Klaus (2020), 'An unsolved cryptogram left behind by poet Edwin Emmanuel Bradford', *Cipherbrain*, at https://scienceblogs.de/klausis-krypto-kolumne/2020/12/03/an-unsolved-cryptogram-left-behind-by-poet-edwin-emmanuel-bradford/ (accessed March 2023).

s.n. [Edward Mark Slocum] (1924), *Men and Boys: An Anthology*, New York. Republished 1978, New York-London: The Coltsfoot Press.

Stevenson, Jane (2003) (first published 1998), 'Nacktleben', in Dominic Montserrat (ed.), *Changing Bodies, Changing Meanings: Studies on the Human Body in Antiquity*, London and New York: Routledge.

Summers, Claude J. (ed.) (2013) (first published 2002), *The Gay & Lesbian Literary Heritage: A Reader's Companion to the Writers and Their Works, from Antiquity to the Present*, Abingdon and New York: Routledge.

Tamagne, Florence (2006) (first published 2000 as *Histoire de l'homosexualité en Europe*), *A History of Homosexuality in Europe. Volume I & II: Berlin, London, Paris 1919-1939*, New York: Algora Publishing.

Taylor, Brian (1976), 'Motives for Guilt-Free Pederasty: Some Literary Considerations', in *Sociological Review*, vol. 24, no. 1, pp. 97-114.

Taylor-Martin, Patrick (1983), *John Betjeman: His Life and Work*, London: Allen Lane.

Trousdale, Rachel (2018), 'Tell Me the Truth: Humor, Love, and Community in Auden's Late 1930s Poetry', in Rachel Trousdale (ed.), *Humor in Modern American Poetry*, New York: Bloomsbury Academic.

Waters, Sarah Ann (1995), *Wolfskins and Togas: Lesbian and Gay Historical Fictions, 1870 to the Present*, London: Queen Mary and Westfield College, University of London (Ph.D. thesis).

Watson, Benjamin (1992), *English Schoolboy Stories: An Annotated Bibliography of Hardcover Fiction*, Metuchen, N.J. and London: The Scarecrow Press, Inc.

Webb, Paul (ed.) (1988), *To Boys Unknown. Poems by Rev. E. E. Bradford*, London: GMP Publishers Ltd.

Webb, P. (27 February 1988), 'Not one is as pretty as he', in *The Spectator*, vol. 260, no. 8329, pp. 14-6.

Willoughby, L. A. (1957), 'Paris in the Nineties', in *Contemporary Review*, vol. 191, no. 1097, pp. 267-73.

Wood, Connor (2021), 'Decoding the Uranian Circle', *Exon* 24, pp. 32-33, at https://www.exeter.ox.ac.uk/inc/uploads/2021/09/exon-21.pdf (accessed March 2023).

Yelton, Michael (2009), *Outposts of the Faith: Anglo-Catholicism in Some Rural Parishes*, Norwich: Canterbury Press.

Young, Ian (1994) (first published 1979), 'The Poetry of Male Love', in Karla Jay and Allen Young (eds.), *Lavender Culture*, New York and London: New York University Press.

Publications by E. E. Bradford

Book publications

- ❖ *Sermon Sketches for the Sundays of the Christian Year: Being Fifty-seven Outline Sermons on Texts Taken from the Sunday Epistles Or Gospels, Together with Addresses for Christmas Day and Good Friday*, London: Skeffington & Son, 1907.
- ❖ *Stories of Life at Our Great Public Schools*, London: Arthur H. Stockwell, 1908.
- ❖ *Sonnets Songs & Ballads*, London: Kegan Paul, Trench, Trübner & Company (Kegan Paul for short), 1908.
- ❖ *Passing the Love of Women and Other Poems*, London: Kegan Paul, 1913.
- ❖ *In Quest of Love and Other Poems*, London: Kegan Paul, 1914.
- ❖ *Lays of Love and Life*, London: Kegan Paul, 1916.
- ❖ *The New Chivalry and Other Poems*, London: Kegan Paul, 1918.
- ❖ *The Romance of Youth and Other Poems*, London: Kegan Paul, 1920.
- ❖ *Ralph Rawdon: A Story in Verse*, London: Kegan Paul, 1922.
- ❖ *The True Aristocracy*, London: Kegan Paul, 1923.
- ❖ *The Tree of Knowledge*, London: Kegan Paul, 1925.
- ❖ *The Kingdom Within You and Other Poems*, London: Kegan Paul, 1927.
- ❖ *Strangers and Pilgrims*, London: Kegan Paul, 1929.
- ❖ *Boyhood*, London: Kegan Paul, 1930.

Book publications edited by third parties

- ❖ *Boris Orloff: A Christmas Yarn*, Stoke Ferry: Daedalus Press, 1968. Limited edition by Timothy d'Arch Smith of 220 copies plus 10 copies on Japanese paper lettered A to J.
- ❖ *To Boys Unknown. Poems by Rev. E. E. Bradford*, London: GMP Publishers Ltd, 1988. Anthology edited by Paul Webb.
- ❖ *St Petersburg Boys*, Portsmouth: Callum James, 2006. Limited edition of 50 copies by Callum James; includes Bradford's stories 'Boris Orloff' and 'The Fete at Peterhof'.
- ❖ *My Love Is Like All Lovely Things: Selected Poems of E. E. Bradford*, London: Arcadian Dreams, 2023. Selected, with an essay on the poet's life and work, by C. Caunter.

Uncollected stories (an incomplete list)

- ❖ 'Boris Orloff', in *The Boy's Own Paper*, vol. XV, nos. 764-5, 2 & 9 September 1893. Reprinted as *Boris Orloff: A Christmas Yarn*, Stoke Ferry: Daedalus Press, 1968. Limited edition by Timothy d'Arch Smith of 220 copies plus 10 copies on Japanese paper lettered A to J. Also reprinted, with the story 'The Fete at Peterhof', in *St Petersburg Boys*, Portsmouth: Callum James, 2006. Limited edition of 50 copies by Callum James.
- ❖ 'A Boy Isvoschik', in the 1895 *Chatterbox* annual.
- ❖ 'Don Quixote's Last Combat', in *The Boy's Own Paper*, vol. XVII, no. 838, 2 February 1895.

❖ 'Love Is for Ever', in *Atalanta* 94, July 1895.

❖ 'What Might Have Been!', in *Atalanta* 99, December 1895.

❖ 'How We Rescued a Slave at Tanjier', in *The Boy's Own Paper*, vol. XVIII, no. 893, 22 February 1896.

❖ 'Our Trip to Mycenæ', in *The Boy's Own Paper*, vol. XVIII, nos. 921-4, 5, 12, 19 & 26 September 1896.

❖ 'My Friend Ismyrlian', in *The Boy's Own Paper*, vol. XIX, no. 958, 22 May 1897.

❖ 'My Rival Basil: An Adventure with the Kabyles', in *The Boy's Own Paper*, summer number for 1898.

❖ 'The Land of the Tsars: A Holiday Adventure', in *The Boy's Own Paper*, vol. XXI, no. 1042, 31 December 1898.

❖ 'An Independent Gentleman', in the 1899 *Chatterbox Christ- mas-box* annual, reprinted in the 1908 *Chatterbox* annual.

❖ 'Heroes and Chimæras. A Story of Modern Greece', in the 1899 *Chatterbox Christmas-box* annual.

❖ 'How We Turned Bedouin Robbers', in *The Boy's Own Paper*, vol. XXII, no. 1099, 3 February 1900, reprinted in *The Montreal Weekly Witness*, 16 December 1902.

❖ 'The Biter Bit', in *The Boy's Own Paper* (Christmas number), 1900.

❖ 'Bear Hunting In Russia and Out of It', in the 1900 *Chatterbox Christmas-box* annual, reprinted in the *County Observer and Monmouthshire Central Advertiser*, 29 December 1900, p. 3.

❖ 'How We Winged a Thessaly Gaol-bird', in *The Boy's Own Paper*, vol. XXIII, no. 1183, 14 September 1901.

❖ 'Yannos and Yankos', in *Goodwill*, 1902.

❖ 'A Dog with a Bad Name', in *The Boy's Own Paper*, vol. XXIV, no. 1210, 22 March 1902.

❖ 'In Fanatic Tangier', in *The Boy's Own Paper*, 1902/1903.

❖ 'Our Treasure-hunt at Sakkara', in *The Boy's Own Paper*, vol. XXVI, no. 1322, 14 May 1904.

- ❖ 'The Fete at Peterhof', in *Sunday Readings for the Young*, 1906. Reprinted, with the story 'Boris Orloff', in *St Petersburg Boys*, Portsmouth: Callum James, 2006. Limited edition of 50 copies by Callum James.
- ❖ 'How to Cure a Fit of the Blues', in *Young Men*, August 1908.

Bear Hunting In Russia and Out of It

A story by E. E. Bradford

"I wish you weren't such a bear!" said my friend Reggie Edwards, not crossly, but in the same quiet tone of voice in which he might have said "I wish the rain would stop."

"I wish *you* weren't such a monkey!" I snapped. "No wonder they call you Monkey at school. You are always up to some stupid monkey trick, you silly little ape."

This didn't ruffle Monkey a bit. He slipped his arm round my shoulder, and rubbed his head gently against mine in a funny caressing way he has—"just like a cat," I say when I'm cross, which is pretty often; and I don't dislike it all the same. "Look here, you old bear," he continued, "I'll give you all my monkey tricks and obey you and be good if you'll promise never to be bearish to me." I am awfully fond of Monkey, though one might not think it from the way in which I sometimes treat him, so I said I would think about it. And the end of it was that we made this compact; and we have only broken it once, and that is what I am going to tell you about.

312

It happens that I have a couple of uncles who live in Russia. Uncle George, who is consul at St. Petersburg, and Uncle Jack, who has married a Russian wife, and lives down in the country at a little place called Berezika, about half-way between St. Petersburg and Moscow. And last Christmas holidays Uncle George invited me to come out and spend them with him, and as he knew that Monkey and I were inseparables, he invited Monkey too. We didn't need to be asked twice! But when we got out there Uncle Jack said we must come down and see him too. This we were not quite so eager to do. The country in winter seemed rather dull, and there were no young people there. We had to go down by night by a horrid slow train, because no other stopped at Berezika, and early in the morning we got out at a little station close to the Valdai Hills (which, by the way, are a swindle—such gentle slopes that you hardly know when you are at the top or when you are at the bottom.) Uncle, who said he would meet us, was late, and there we stood in the icy air, with nothing but snow and pine trees to be seen, shivering in our furs. I wished myself back at St. Petersburg, and said so.

When at last Uncle Jack turned up with the sledge, it was not a jolly great three-horsed troika as I had expected, but what he called a Finnish sledge, a wretched little square wooden box drawn by a single horse. Uncle Jack and I sat in front, and Monkey behind, and what must that stupid boy do but slip a great snowball between the collar of my *shuba* and my fur cap. I didn't notice it till it began to melt and trickle down my back, and then it was too late.

At the end of a fearful long drive through an apparently endless pine forest, we came to the house. It wasn't cold indoors, though there was no fire to be seen, only gigantic white china stoves built into the wall. But it was so stuffy and smelly that it took away all my appetite. Then, the lunch was so nasty! It began with cabbage soup, which wasn't so bad, but after I had taken a few mouthfuls Aunt said, "You should put some cream in it, my

313

dear!" And before I could refuse, that idiot Monkey plumped in a regular lot of sour cream, and completely spoilt it. After the soup we had some gluey patties made of fish and isinglass—horrid things! These were followed by cold boiled sucking-pig, ugh! while a sweet buckwheat pudding brought up the rear.

Directly after lunch, Uncle and Aunt calmly drove off to see a friend who was ill, and lived a long way off, telling us to amuse ourselves till dinner time. I felt very cross, I can tell you. And what made it all the more trying for me was the fact that Monkey seemed to be in the best of spirits, and found everything "an awful lark!"

"Let's go out and have a battle of snowballing," he said. I didn't object to this, partly because I was glad to get out of the hot, fusty house, and partly because I thought this was a good chance of letting off a little of my temper. I banged away at Monkey with all my might, till he had to dodge behind the trees to avoid my shots. But in this way he kept getting further and further from the house.

"Come back!" I shouted, after a bit. "Come back, you duffer!"

"Oh, I daresay!" he laughed. "Don't you wish you may get it? I'm not going back to be shot at!" and flinging at me five or six balls which he had ready, he ran hard off again, and hid behind the trees. And he kept going on like this until we were fairly lost. He got serious enough then. We knew that the forest extended for miles and miles, and night was fast coming on.

"Now all this comes of your not obeying orders. You promised to obey me and be good!" I said angrily.

But Monkey couldn't let this pass without a protest even now. "I only promised to obey you if you gave up being bearish to me!" he replied. But before I had time to make any answer we heard the report of a gun! It sounded as if it were at no great distance, so we ran in the direction from which it seemed to come, shouting at the top of our voices to attract the attention of the sportsmen. Presently two other shots followed in quick succession, and then—never shall I forget it!—we saw an enormous bear quite close, and making straight for us! We swarmed up one of the pine trees as fast as ever we could go, full of blind terror, for we had not the faintest idea whether the bear could climb up after us or not!

But happily our fears were soon over.

The poor brute had already been wounded, for its blood was fast dropping on the snow; and in a few moments another well aimed shot put it—and us—out of misery. The hunters came up, and as one of them spoke a little English, and knew where our Uncle lived, we soon got back safe and sound.

But Monkey is incorrigible.

"You see what it is!" he cried to me in tones of glee, "you'll have to hunt that old bear of a temper of yours—for if you don't hunt the bear, the bear will hunt you!"

Index of titles and first lines

Titles of poems are in roman; first lines are in italics.

Printed in Dunstable, United Kingdom

64518637R10190